The Portuguese Nun

MARIANA ALCOFORADO
A freira portuguesa

An anonymous etching of the Portuguese Nun reproduced in José Cerqueira de Vasconcelos, *As Cartas de Religiosa Portuguesa* (Lisboa, 1935).

The Portuguese Nun

Formation of a National Myth

Anna Klobucka

Lewisburg
Bucknell University Press
London: Associated University Presses

Associated University Presses
440 Forsgate Drive
Cranbury, NJ 08512

Associated University Presses
16 Barter Street
London WC1A 2AH, England

Associated University Presses
P.O. Box 338, Port Credit
Mississauga, Ontario
Canada L5G 4L8

The paper used in this publication meets the requirements of the American National Standard for Permanence of Paper for Printed Library Materials Z39.48-1984.

Library of Congress Cataloging-in-Publication Data

Klobucka, Anna, 1961–
    The Portuguese nun : formation of a national myth / Anna Klobucka.
        p. cm.
    Includes bibliographical references and index.
    ISBN 0–8387–5465–1 (alk. paper)
    1. Guilleragues, Gabriel Joseph de Lavergne, vicomte de, 1628–1685. Lettres portugaises. 2. Guilleragues, Gabriel Joseph de Lavergne, vicomte de, 1628–1685—Translations into Portuguese. 3. Literature and society—Portugal. I. Title.

    PQ1799.G795 L4339 2000
    843'.4—dc21

                                                                    00–034224

Contents

Acknowledgments

A NUMBER OF GENEROUS INSTITUTIONS AND NO LESS GENEROUS INDIVIDUALS helped make this book a reality. The Sarah H. Moss Fellowship I received from the University of Georgia in the summer of 1995 allowed me to carry out the necessary initial research in Portugal. The Center for Humanities and Arts, also at the University of Georgia, granted me one of its Research Fellowships at the precise time when it was most needed for timely completion of the manuscript. I also thank the Portuguese Biblioteca Nacional in Lisbon for the permission to use illustrations reproduced from its holdings and for the prompt and efficient processsing of my requests. Assembleia Distrital of Beja was similarly gracious in allowing me to reproduce the photograph of the "Mértola Window," a crucial image in the story told in this book.

Among the friends and colleagues with whom I shared this project I wish to single out Hilary Owen for her unfailing assistance and encouragement. Many thanks to all those who read all or parts of this manuscript: Luis Correa-Díaz, Dimitar Kambourov, Susan Quinlan, Ian Rutherford, Brigitte Weltman-Aron, and Richard Zenith. I also thank Jonathan Krell for assisting me with translations from the French, and, lastly, Victor Mendes for phone calls to Beja and all the rest.

The Portuguese Nun

Prologue: What Really Happened

FIRST PUBLISHED IN 1669 IN PARIS, THE ANONYMOUS *Lettres portugaises traduites en françois* presented itself, through an introductory *avis au lecteur*, as an equally anonymous translation of five authentic love letters written by a Portuguese nun named "Marianne." The nun, cloistered in a provincial convent in the southeastern part of Portugal, addressed them to an (unnamed) officer in the French army who for a while had been stationed in her town, during which time a secret love affair developed between the two. The Frenchman's departure ended the romance, but in no way diminished the intensity of the abandoned nun's passionate feelings for her ex-lover. It is about those feelings that she wrote to him in exuberant yet masterful prose, worthy of the most accomplished literary craftsmen of the French *grand siècle*. Soon after their publication, the letters became an international bestseller. The same year, two pirated editions followed, one in Cologne, the other one in Amsterdam, both with somewhat altered titles over nearly identical text (one twist brought into play by the Cologne edition was its naming both of the nun's lover and of the alleged translator of her letters).[1] The original publisher, Claude Barbin, retaliated by issuing, still in 1669, another printing of the first edition, a second edition, and a sequel containing additional letters, even as yet another pirated version was being brought out in Dijon. Two more printings followed in 1670 and a third edition in 1672 (Alcover 1985, 644). The first English translation, by Roger L'Estrange, entitled *Five Love Letters From A Nun To A Cavalier Done Out Of The French Into English* appeared in 1678, and over the following decades and indeed centuries, countless translations, imitations, and purported sequels and responses to the original five letters kept alive the story of the provincial Portuguese nun seduced and abandoned by her aristocratic French lover. To write "à la portugaise" became "a veritable code for a certain style—written at the height of passion in a moment of disorder and distress" (Kauffman 1986, 95). Stendhal pointed

11

to the Portuguese Nun as one of the prototypes for his "amour-passion" (1959, 5), and it has been suggested that Elizabeth Barrett Browning's acclaimed *Sonnets from the Portuguese* owed much of their inspiration to this seventeenth-century classic of amorous discourse (Monteiro 1996, 32–34). More recently, the designation "le type portugais" has been proposed as a formal category by critics studying the development and characteristics of the epistolary genre in European literary tradition (Jost 1968, 144–46).[2]

Part of the appeal exercised by the nun's letters has been due of course to the titillating uncertainty surrounding the factual identity of their author. The debate on that issue started in earnest in the early nineteenth century when a French scholar, Jean-François Boissonade, published a note identifying the nun as one "Mariana Alcaforada" and the town where her convent was located as Beja, the main municipality of the Portuguese province of Lower Alentejo.[3] It is interesting to note that this first appearance of the nun's full name—until then she had been referred to variously as "a Portuguese religious," "a Portuguese lady," or even, incongruously, as "a canoness from Lisbon"—postdated by a mere few years the invention of the legal fiction of the author as an individual bearing specific, protected rights. The law of 19 July 1793, which had proclaimed "the declaration of the rights of genius," for the first time acknowledged authors' claims of property with regard to their texts (Hesse 1986, 8). It is similarly worth observing that Boissonade also distinguished himself as an important and unorthodox champion of the Greek poet Sappho, demonstrating, in the words of Joan DeJean, "a consistent involvement with questions of the legitimacy of women's writing" (1989, 348).

Curiously enough, for the first century and a half of their existence the international notoriety of the letters provoked no response whatsoever in their presumed country of origin. As most authors suggest, this was probably due to the censorship exercised in Portugal by the Inquisition: it is significant that the only mention of the work to be found in writings of a Portuguese writer prior to the nineteenth century came from the pen of the cosmopolitan aristocrat Cavalheiro de Oliveira, who converted to Anglicanism, wrote in French and Italian, and spent most of his life abroad (Rodrigues 1935, 124). The first translations of the letters into what was assumed to be their original idiom were likewise brought forth by Portuguese expatriates, respectively in 1819 by Filinto Elísio and in 1825 by José Maria de Sousa Botelho (also referred to by his aristocratic title of Morgado de Mateus). Both translations were published in Paris, but in subsequent years they did become disseminated in Portugal, inaugurating an independent process of reception and interpretation, which gradually led to the development of one of the country's most cherished cultural myths.

The slow but steady growth of interest in Mariana Alcoforado and her epistolary masterpiece, which took place in Portugal throughout the nineteenth century, was paralleled by a relative stagnation of critical involvement on the French side. While it was a Frenchman, *l'abbé* Mercier de Saint-Léger who, in the last years of the eighteenth century, published what it generally cited as the first scholarly study of the letters (*Notice historique et bibliographique sur les Lettres portugaises*, included in the 1796 edition by Delance), the nineteenth-century Portuguese researches into the presumed historical context of their production dominated the scene of the text's interpretation, with few significant contributions arriving from other quarters until the second decade of the twentieth century.[4] Most notably, it was discovered that a nun by the name of Maria Ana (Mariana) Alcoforado had in fact lived in the convent of Conceição in Beja and was in her mid to late twenties at the time when the French contingent, headed by the Count of Schomberg, took part in the Portuguese War of Restoration against Spain (Beja being the center of military operations in the years 1666–68). Notwithstanding the scarcity of tangible documentary evidence, as well as the absence of any Portuguese manuscript that could be presented as the original of the French "translation" of the letters, the case for the authenticity of both the love affair and the resulting correspondence appeared reasonably well established.

In 1926, in an article published in *The Modern Language Review*, entitled "Who Was the Author of the *Lettres portugaises*?," F. C. Green, then a professor of French literature in Rochester, New York, reopened the authorship debate. Based on his examination of the original *Privilège du Roi* granted to the publisher Claude Barbin in 1668, Green concluded that the "Cuilleraque" mentioned in the first pirated edition as the translator of the letters was in fact their legitimate author, although he hesitated to identify him firmly with the courtier, diplomat, and onetime French ambassador to Constantinople, Gabriel-Joseph de Lavergne de Guilleragues. That identification would, however, be supported and substantiated by further studies, most notably by Frédéric Deloffre's and Jacques Rougeot's introduction to their edition of *Lettres portugaises, Valentins et autres oeuvres de Guilleragues* (Paris: Garnier, 1962), followed ten years later by a revised and supplemented *édition nouvelle*, in which the extended argument in favor of the French author's "paternity" of the letters, declared as no longer necessary, was replaced by a simply constative account of their history, and a "life of Guilleragues" found "its natural place at the head of [his] work" (Guilleragues 1972, vii). Few scholars have since questioned what is now the widely shared consensus regarding Guilleragues's authorship and the fictional nature of the *Lettres portugaises* with their artifice of *dépaysement* foreshadowing the use of the same device in such later works as Montesquieu's *Lettres persanes* (1721) or Mme de Grafigny's *Lettres d'une Péruvienne* (1747).[5]

Such has been, summarily, the history of the text. As for the history of the events that conspired to bring the *Lettres portugaises* into existence, it is far less clear what had really happened. Did Noel Bouton de Chamilly (or another Frenchman) ever meet Mariana Alcoforado (or another Portuguese nun) sometime in 1666 or 1667 in Beja? Did a secret liaison take place in the Convento da Conceição (or in another convent) and was a nun abandoned by a soldier against her desire? Did anybody write any love letters, or even any "authentic" letters at all, in either Portuguese or French, before Guilleragues (or another writer) showed up at Claude Barbin's Parisian doorstep, at the second *perron* of Sainte Chapelle, with a promising manuscript in hand? Compelling as these questions have been for generations of scholars, as well as for scores of amateur inquiring minds (including my own), I will make no effort to address them in this book. Steering away from the question of factual authorship, I will instead consider the *Lettres portugaises* as the multilayered cultural artifact they have become since their seventeenth-century inception, a text whose meaning has been construed through the long and complex history of its diverse interpretations and debates concerning its origin. Such a reorientation of critical concerns is of course hardly a novelty: most recent readings of the *Lettres* have been influenced by the paradigm shift from validation toward signification occurring in the postmodern context, writers and critics alike choosing to focus on the meaning of a particular text or event rather than on the determination of its truth value. Already in 1954, the opening paragraph of Leo Spitzer's seminal and widely influential interpretation of the *Lettres* made explicit that its premise involved moving away from the question (as asked earlier by F. C. Green), "Who was the author of the *Lettres portugaises*?," and toward "an intrinsically much more important question . . . : 'What is the meaning of the *Lettres portugaises*?'" (Spitzer 1988, 255). This self-consciously groundbreaking change of direction notwithstanding, it has to be pointed out that the issue of authorship retained for Spitzer much of the overwhelming importance that it had held for his predecessors (and would still hold, after all, for many of his acknowledged followers), becoming merely deferred to the aftermath of the critic's demonstration of the text's "correctly established meaning": "As long as the work itself remains ill-defined, its causative force (the author's personality) must be for ever obscure" (255). Spitzer's peremptorily conclusive portrayal of that personality as belonging to a (male French) "author who knew his business" (281) well enough to give his despairing heroine "abundant cartesian lucidity and a language . . . redolent with the literary nobility of French prose of the classical period" (283) heralded both future attribution of the *Lettres* to Guilleragues and, unforeseeably and somewhat further down the road, dissenting critiques voiced by feminist literary scholars who denounced as preconceived and transparently stereotyped the notions of gender underlying and legitimating Spitzer's argument.[6]

As a canonical text of French literature that continues to invite and stimulate critical attention, the *Lettres portugaises* have supported an array of interpretations as numerous as they are varied (as of this writing, a title search of the MLA Bibliography database produces eighty items, ranging from brief notes to doctoral dissertations and books, that in one way or another deal with the text). However, whether concerned primarily with the attribution of its authorship or with its intrinsic and/or contextual meaning, readings of the *Lettres portugaises* undertaken on the international scholarly scene have not so far taken into account a highly complex life of their own that the text and the imagined figure of its protagonist and presumed author gradually came to acquire in their supposed country of origin. Therefore, while adopting as an incidental working premise the generally accepted thesis of French authorship, I will also direct my attention away from France and toward Portugal: for it is there that the story of Mariana Alcoforado's misfortunate passion and epistolary triumph has, over the last two centuries, found the most fertile ground in the national imagination, turning the (real) country of her (fictional) origin into a truly fascinating space of cultural invention and intervention.[7] Thus, while the story of the Portuguese Nun can be (and has been) told in many ways, the narrative I have chosen to compose may be described as an account of an elaborate enterprise of cultural mythmaking, spanning a couple of centuries and involving such diverse methodologies as bona fide historical research, novelistic fantasy, political argument, and at least one remarkable instance of a postmodern blending of all of the above. The elusive "Marianne" whose complaint arises from the pages of the *Lettres portugaises* remained, for the first century and a half of her existence, an anonymous, virtually disembodied textual shadow, infinitely appealing but at the same time irretrievably remote, defined solely by the geographic circumstances of her exotic (dis)placement. It was through the efforts of generations of Portuguese *alcoforadistas* that she became gradually fleshed out, given a personal identity and a genealogy, both familial and national, that shaped her not merely into a fully formed mythical figure, but also into a nationally representative epitome of femininity and, by a uniquely Portuguese extension, of national identity in general.

1

Love and Paranoia on a Cultural Periphery

THE PORTUGUESE NUN HAS BEEN PAINTED IN A GREAT VARIETY OF GUISES by her many interpreters and the *Lettres portugaises* have retained a steady presence, occasionally even becoming a focus of lively debates, in the referential canon of international literary scholarship. One of the features of this favorable critical fortune of the text, particularly in the twentieth century, has been, however, the gradual emptying of its constitutive *appellation d'origine* of any claims to referential rooting in a national specificity. At the same time, the contentious question of its male or female authorship has more or less remained at the forefront of analysis, particularly since it was brought into theoretically and ideologically sharpened focus by feminist criticism. Simply put, discussions of the text on the international scene have typically focused on the issue of its author's gender, eschewing or marginalizing the question of his or her nationality. On the other hand, by a perhaps inescapable contrast, the Portuguese tradition has always intimately linked both aspects, inscribing the mythical figure of "Soror Mariana" within the literary and cultural history of the nation. The national attribution of authorship, an issue of secondary importance, at best, to the vast international majority of readers and critics of the seventeenth-century text, has assumed and retained in Portugal a degree of prominence that clearly points to its continuing investment in the fabrication, by the country's cultural elites, of what Benedict Anderson has described as a shared "national imagination" (1991, 30).

Discovering and investigating the voluminous body of writing penned by Portuguese enthusiasts of Soror Mariana (as well as by a substantial minority opposed to her inclusion in the national canon) has been a fascinating enterprise, not least because of the sheer variety of discourses that in one way or another center on the Portuguese Nun. To give but a few preliminary examples, there are several book-length biographies, ranging from scholarly to frankly novelistic in style and substance; chapters in literary histories; poems and plays; a modernist manifesto; a study by a pioneering practitioner of sexual medicine entitled *Psychological Maso-chism of Soror Mariana* and originally published in the *Archives of Legal Medicine*. Generation after generation, legions of *alcoforadistas* of the most diverse stripe have attempted to write Mariana into existence, to de-cipher the material reality of her female body and the cultural identity of her Portuguese voice in the rhetorical cadences of the letters.

What follows is an account of that myth and its formation, set against the complex background of nineteenth- and twentieth-century Portuguese culture and politics, or, more precisely, politics of culture. Informed by what Louis Montrose describes as the post-structuralist "reciprocal con-cern with the historicity of texts and the textuality of history" and by the privileging of "histories" over "History" (1989, 20), this project can be sit-uated in the theoretical vicinity of the New Historicist critical enterprise, insofar as it also seeks to "eschew overarching hypothetical constructs in favor of surprising coincidences" and is "less concerned to project long-range trajectories than to note bizarre overlappings" and to "evoke unsuspected borrowings and lendings among activities, institutions, and archives . . . previously held to be independent and unrelated," demon-strating that "social and cultural events commingle messily" (Veeser 1989, xii). In the story of Mariana Alcoforado, such unsuspected borrowings, bizarre overlappings, and messy comminglings can be detected through-out. To cite just one prominent example, the 1888 publication of Luciano Cordeiro's groundbreaking study *Soror Mariana* is shown here to be "overlapping" with its author's lifelong career as the founder of the Lisbon Geographical Society and a staunch defender of Portuguese inter-ests in Africa, and the book's enthusiastic reception is seen to "com-mingle" with public upheaval brought about by the crisis of the so-called British Ultimatum. Nevertheless, I am also guided by the belief that the gaudy attractiveness of such an anecdotal collage should not seduce one away from heeding Elizabeth Fox-Genovese's warning against the futility of indiscriminate antiquarianism (as opposed to history, "at least good his-tory," which, as Fox-Genovese points out, is always structural) (1989, 217). An orgy of carnivalesque free associating is all too likely to swallow an innocent observer of Mariana's story: like a postmodern novel waiting to be written, it therefore requires a plot, however convoluted, and some sort of discursive unity-in-fragments, however inconclusive and multi-directional.

As it happens, Fox-Genovese's caveat, in spite of distinct cultural and ideological coordinates of its own, bears considerable resemblance to the arguments put forward in the Portuguese sociologist Boaventura de Sousa Santos's important, manifesto-like text "Onze teses por ocasião de mais uma descoberta de Portugal" (1994, 49–67).[1] In his "eleven theses," Sousa Santos denounces the "mythic excess of interpretation" characteristic of Portuguese nationalist discourse, product of a culture "without a philo-sophical or scientific tradition" and a "compensatory mechanism" reacting against a "deficit of reality" (49).[2] Not only are cultural myths themselves arbitrary and selective in their demagogic manipulation of past and present social and historical realities: any analysis or commentary that uncritically confronts the myth on its own terrain is likely to affirm its universal postu-lates and perpetuate its power to "transform history into nature" (Barthes 1987, 129). As Sousa Santos points out, arbitrary analysis—akin to Fox-Genovese's antiquarianism—"replicates the myth, even when intention-ally attempting to deconstruct it" (51). The mythic discourse of Portuguese cultural nationalism must be therefore "considered a sociological phe-nomenon in its own right and analyzed as such" (75). It should be noted, however, that while what is at stake for the American historian in opposing "antiquarianism" is, at most, what she perceives as a danger of intellectual sloppiness and academic illegitimacy, for the Portuguese sociologist the perils are of a much higher order, involving politically influential symbolic definition of the nation and the articulation of Portuguese national(ist) dis-course at the country's historical crossroads. In seeking to substitute ana-lytic apparatus of social sciences for the circular logic of mythic exegesis, his effort may also be related to Eric Hobsbawm's and Terence Ranger's implication, in their demystification of "invented traditions," that properly applied historical apparatus will serve to expose those constructs as little more than extravagant instruments of ideological false consciousness, whose superficial legitimacy must not be confused with "the strength and adaptability of genuine traditions" (1983, 8).

The Portuguese myth of Soror Mariana Alcoforado is an invented tradi-tion *par excellence*.[3] It was a product of nineteenth- and twentieth-century nationalist revival, whose genuinely historical (as well as pseudo-historical) references were sought after and established *ex post facto* through largely fictitious claims of continuity. It arose as other invented traditions have, through historical opportunism masquerading as timeless authenticity: "In short, they are responses to novel situations which take the form of refer-ence to old situations, or which establish their own past by quasi-obligatory repetition" (Hobsbawm and Ranger 1983, 2). On the other hand, however, the story of the Portuguese Nun also illustrates the possibility, unfortu-nately de-emphasized in Hobsbawm's analysis, that once formulated and brought into the realm of public discourse, such "traditions" do not always remain stagnated and bound in their original ideological straightjackets, but often become capable of developing a symbolic vitality all their own, at which point an operative distinction between "genuine" and "invented" traditions proves somewhat less than useful. A particularly forceful demonstration of this claim may be found in the example of the feminist manifesto *Novas Cartas Portuguesas* (1972), collectively authored by Maria Isabel Barreno, Maria Teresa Horta, and Maria Velho da Costa, whose revisionist interpretation of Soror Mariana's story, similarly to many other rewritings of established narratives from a previously marginalized perspective, propelled the myth in new and exciting directions. Restituting the past not in terms of a truth to recover, but as a richly suggestive source of historical and symbolic substance, the "Three Marias" did not set out to "demythify" Mariana, but rather enlisted her in their progressive enterprise, which encompassed both a direct description and denunciation of social and historical realities lived by Portuguese women and a compensatory semiotic remythification of one of the most prominent fictions of Portuguese womanhood.

To be sure, most individual instances of the *alcoforadista* (as well as anti-*alcoforadista*) discourse produced in Portugal since the early nineteenth century are not nearly as remarkable as *Novas Cartas Portuguesas*. However, when taken as a whole, and particularly when pitched against each other, they constitute a formidable exercise in nationalist imagology, a rich and inspiring repository of evidence towards a critical analysis of "the processes by which the nation came to be imagined and, once imagined, modeled, adapted and transformed" (Anderson 1991, 141).[4] In fact, the myth of Soror Mariana provides a singularly apt basis for a case study in which nearly all of the major themes of Portuguese national imagination have been developed and negotiated. It is only from a perspective that narrowly equates historical invention with fabrication and falsity that a summary rejection of Portuguese *alcoforadista* discourse may be effected, although it is equally true that the "irritating mix of mystery and evidence" (Pageaux 1983, 93) found in the story both contributes to its complexity and makes it difficult for a potential participant to assume a coolly disinvested scholarly stance. For the very debate on the issue of the letters' authenticity and national legitimacy has traditionally proceeded along the lines of an uncompromising search for historical truth pitting itself against purveyance of pleasing and plausible fiction, with an attendant rhetoric pitching "reason" against "emotion," "professors" against "poets," and so forth. To complicate matters further, the position of privileging and defending historical accuracy has been, naturally if somewhat ironically, assumed by those who claim the *Lettres portugaises* to be a literary fake, by the proponents of its fictional literariness; while, on the other hand, the believers in the historically authentic origin of the letters have been forced, by the scarcity and unreliability of their evidence, to couch their convictions in terms of fictional discourse, rewriting the disjointed and occasionally self-contradictory record as a coherent narrative with a beginning (the love affair), the all-important middle (the abandoned Mariana's creative despair), and the rather anticlimactic resolution (the nun's long, penitent life and Chamilly's distinguished, if unexceptional, military career). Thus the entire corpus of *alcoforadista* and anti-*alcoforadista* writing not only oscillates between the competing claims of history and fiction, but often either directly addresses or indirectly dramatizes their (in)compatibility.

Of course, such precariously unstable epistemological status is a condition shared by many foundational myths of modern nationality, in Portugal and elsewhere. As Perry Anderson notes, the construction of any national identity is a selective process (in contrast to the more comprehensive and inclusive concept of national character). This is precisely what gives the end product its inherent fragility: resulting from a "projection of a few selected features of historical experience onto an emblematic plane" it is prone "to a kind of structural anxiety" (1991, 7–8). In the case of Soror Mariana, when elevated to the status of a nationally representative image, such anxiety has become exacerbated almost to the breaking point (and in some cases beyond it), since the inscription of the nun's conflicted love story into the mythical canon of Portuguese culture has always, by necessity, presented itself as a highly ambivalent task. After all, to quote Eduardo Lourenço's succinct exegesis of the dilemma, the lovesick writer of the *Lettres* speaks in "[a] mais portuguesa voz," the most Portuguese of voices, that is, at the same time, "uma ficção reexportada de França," a fiction reexported from France (1977, 10). Even at the time when the work's Portuguese authorship stood as a widely accepted given, it was impossible to ignore the constitutive role played by variously imagined agents of foreignness in the making of one of the most cherished representations of national sameness: be it as a writer (Guilleragues) or as a soldier (Chamilly), the seductive French accomplice of Mariana's infidelity to her physically and symbolically circumscribed double closure of conventual confinement and national allegiance has remained centrally poised within her story, disrupting or, indeed, invalidating a priori the narcissistic ritual of patriotic self-absorption encouraged by considerations of other, less questionable, mythical icons of national identity.

It is no wonder therefore that although the thesis of Mariana's historical authenticity, as both Chamilly's illicit lover and the true author of the *Lettres portugaises*, for many decades tended to be dominant in Portugal, the debate always accommodated a vocal minority of dissenters, many of whom objected against the nationalistic mythification of the nun on the very same grounds of patriotic pride and loyalty trodden by the legions of her devotees. Thus, one counterargument went, it was at best foolish and at worst downright treasonous to insist on national appropriation of the sinful nun's epistolary lament; while its "sadistic impudence" would not appear out of place in "the gallant France" of Louis XIV (Pereira 1941, 30), it disagreed profoundly with the properly Portuguese, that is, silent and dignified, ways of dealing with sin and atonement:

> Those Portuguese nuns who had become disgraced always knew how to preserve, in the silence of their embittered souls, watered by tears of remorse and penitence, an immense longing for their lost innocence. (21)

It is interesting to observe, in this context, that depictions of Mariana Alcoforado in Portuguese editions of the *Lettres* have in general been subdued and decorous, presenting the unfortunate nun in an attitude of soulful penitence and without such attributes of her passion as those found in her best known French images: pen and paper, a medallion presumably containing Chamilly's likeness, or disheveled dress, all situating Mariana at the climax of her creative despair. In fact, the very scarcity of her Portuguese representations, along with their undramatic appearance, stands in contrast to both the abundance and rhetorical exuberance of written commentary. Likewise, no statues of Soror Mariana are to be found in Portugal; even in Beja, where the nun's memory is often presented as her hometown's main tourist attraction, the figure greeting visitors to what remains of the Convento da Conceição is that of the saintly Queen Leonor, the founder of the convent (on the other hand, glossy brochures available from the local *Turismo* office never mention Queen Leonor, unequivocally promoting Mariana to the status of the convent's most prominent celebrity). All this evidence (or lack thereof) points to the elusiveness of Soror Mariana's presence/absence in the collective Portuguese imaginary and to the nature of her myth as a distinctly non-monumental manifestation of national essence.

However, as I wish to argue, it is precisely this shifting, ambivalent, and often self-contradictory nature of the Portuguese Nun's story that has contributed to its lasting appeal: malleable enough to serve widely differing interests, it has been summoned to support arguments ranging all over the ideological spectrum of Portuguese cultural discourse.[5] Moreover, its conflicting parameters have proven uniquely congruous with the equally discordant characteristics of the nation's modern self-consciousness as it has taken shape from the mid-nineteenth century onward. In his influential essay *O labirinto da saudade* (1978), subtitled "Mythic psychoanalysis of Portuguese destiny," and described as an exercise in national imagology, or "a critical discourse on the images that we have produced of ourselves," Eduardo Lourenço characterized that self-consciousness as determined by a schizophrenic conjunction of the complexes of inferiority and superiority: "According to the contingencies of international or global reality, one of the complexes may prevail, but more frequently both emerge at the same time, the one as a mirror image of the other" (19).

As the most illustrious among the many contemporary Portuguese essayists who have engaged in mythic exegeses of national identity, Lourenço is frequently addressed and critiqued in Boaventura de Sousa Santos's already cited "Eleven Theses."[6] However, notwithstanding his oppositional stance with regard to Lourenço and other national mythographers, as well as the distinct disciplinary postulates of his manifesto, Sousa Santos also claims that Portugal's contradictory status on the global geopolitical scene has constituted "the fundamental structuring aspect" (59) of modern Portuguese collective existence. Portugal was the only colonizing country to be considered, by other colonizing countries, as a "native" or "savage" land. At the same time as Portuguese travelers, soldiers, and diplomats described curious habits and ways of life of the "primitive" peoples they encountered in the process of building the empire, British or French travelers, soldiers, and diplomats described, with curiosity or contempt, the habits and ways of life of the Portuguese, strange for them to such an extent as to appear little less than savage. As Sousa Santos suggests, it is in this duplicity of images and representations that the allegedly "mysterious" coexistence in the Portuguese national consciousness of, on the one hand, an inferiority complex with regard to foreigners and, on the other, a "mythical hypertrophy" generating megalomanias and chimeras may be found (59–60).

Such persistent ambivalence may be explained, according to Sousa Santos, by resorting to the concept of semiperipheral development, originally proposed and theorized within the larger framework of economic and political analysis of the "world-system," most fully and influentially fostered by Immanuel Wallerstein (1974, 1979). Affirming itself initially through criticism of the "developmentalist" perspective in social science, which adopted "society" in the abstract as the theoretical unit for the study of social change and conceived of the world at large as a loose conglomerate of related but basically autonomous "societies," each following on its own terms an essentially similar path of internal development, the world-system perspective has developed on the basis of an oppositional premise: "that the arena within which social action takes place and social change occurs is not 'society' in the abstract, but a definite 'world', a spatio-temporal whole, whose spatial scope is coextensive with the elementary division of labor among its constituent regions or parts and whose temporal scope extends for as long as the elementary division of labor continually reproduces the 'world' as a social whole" (Hopkins, Wallerstein, et al. 1982, 42). The constituent parts of the world-system are organized spatially on a scale of centers and hinterlands, whose extremities are conceptualized, respectively, as "core" and "periphery."[7] The relational character of "coreness" and "peripherality" is among the basic tenets of world-system analysis: the core is defined by its periphery, just as much as the periphery is defined by its core, and in fact it is the core-periphery *relation* itself that becomes the major focus of attention (Hopkins 1982, 20). Another important point is the recognition that "core" and "periphery" have functioned in actual analyses of different aspects of the modern world-system not just as nouns but also as adjectives (core areas and peripheral areas, core products and peripheral products, core states and peripheral states), and that the resulting distinct units of analysis are by no means homologous or coextensive in their respective positions on the conceptual scale bracketed by the twin poles of core and periphery, producing, instead of a flat, cartographic blueprint, a three-dimensional quasi-holographic image of the world that is composed of overlapping "multiple layers of coreness and peripherality" (Wallerstein 1982, 92), layers whose relative positioning can in addition be said to exist in a state of perpetual mutability.[8]

A particularly interesting zone of the multidimensional global picture projected by world-system analysts is that designated as the semiperiphery. Obviously derivative from the core-periphery dyad, semiperiphery is nevertheless conceptualized as a distinct third category, characterized primarily by its "in-betweenness" on the world-economic scale: "Looking at the world economy as a whole, some states are clearly 'in-between' in the core-periphery structure, in that they house within their borders (in adjacent but often unrelated sectors) both peripheral processes in relation to core states and core-like processes in relation to adjacent peripheral states" (Hopkins, Wallerstein, et al. 1982, 47). Since the category of semiperiphery does not exercise a qualitative impact on the analytic structuring of core-periphery relations, referring instead "to a quantification of such relations as they fall within the bounds of a given state," it follows that the usefulness of the concept lies primarily in isolating a zone of political—as opposed to strictly economic—analysis (Wallerstein 1985, 34–36). Furthermore, as Christopher Chase-Dunn has argued, semiperipheral location appears to favor the development of politically and socially interesting phenomena and can consequently be considered to occupy "a structural position which often has developmental (or evolutionary) significance": "The semiperiphery is seen as a fertile ground for social, organizational and technical innovation and as a strategic location for upward mobility and the establishment of new centers of resource control" (1988, 31).

In addition, as Hopkins and Wallerstein have recognized, a third integral aspect of world-historical development is the role played in it by "a multiplicity of interrelated . . . *cultural communities*—language communities, religious communities, ethnic communities, races, status groups, class communities, scientific communities, and so forth," whose constitution, transformation, and disintegration "form a fundamental set of processes in their own right" (1982, 43; my emphasis). However, the promising interdisciplinary expansion of the world-system perspective's original grounding in political economy proves to be a challenging enterprise, whose progress is affected by the consciousness of difficulties inherent in conceptualizing "the relationships between different kinds of networks of interconnectedness" (Chase-Dunn 1988, 30) that have historically organized processes of intersocietal exchange.[9] Wallerstein's own recent forays into the exploration of what he labels "geoculture" have testified to his understandable interest in exploring these processes as primarily ideological formations; culture, as the "idea-system" of capitalist world economy, "is the outcome of our collective historical attempts to come to terms with the contradictions, the ambiguities, the complexities of the socio-political realities of this particular system" (1991, 166). His considerations tend however to narrow that broad field of inquiry to a more specific and idiosyncratic concept of a "geoculture" essentially akin to the classic Marxist understanding of ideology as false consciousness: it is "the set of values and basic rules that, both consciously and subconsciously, govern reward within the system and create a set of illusions that tend to persuade members to accept the legitimacy of the system" (1995, 146). While the ideological dimension of any cultural system—and of minor, marginal, or peripheral cultural formations in particular—is something I accept as an implicit given, this study relies rather on the broader and more neutral understanding of ideologies in the anthropological (Geertzian) sense, as "systems of interacting symbols, as patterns of interworking meanings" that "transform sentiment into significance" (Geertz 1973, 207) by producing "maps of problematic social reality and matrices for the creation of collective conscience" (220). Since the ideological goals and implications of cultural phenomena discussed here coincide with manifestations of nationalist (or antinationalist) politics, it is worth pointing out that the Geertzian understanding of ideology evoked above is also operative in Benedict Anderson's influential recasting of nationalism as a complex cultural artefact, deployable in multiple and often contradictory ways in a great variety of social contexts, "to merge and be merged with a correspondingly wide variety of political cultural manifestations" (1991, 4).

Theorists seeking to conceptualize cultural and social formations of the European periphery have often followed analytic pathways parallel to the direction proposed by Boaventura de Sousa Santos. David Lloyd, in his complex analyses of the historical construction of Irish national literature and cultural identity, has been guided, similarly to the Portuguese sociologist, by the conviction that "the question of identity has to be rethought not in terms of any ontological or ethnic determination . . . , but in terms of the function of this insistently *unanswerable* question in the assimilation of subjects as citizens for the state" (1993, 5; original emphasis). Lloyd's Ireland and its "anomalous states" have much in common with the modern Portuguese scenario, not least the saturation of the country's discursive field by the theme of identity and the pervasive "perception of self-estrangement, of being perceived and perceiving through alien media" (1–2), an aspect to which I will return. Most crucially, however, unique as specific historical, social, and cultural conditions may be, respectively, in Portugal and in Ireland, the "anomalous" duplicity of national imagination has been in both cases contingent on semiperipheral uncertainty of their geopolitical and geocultural status: metropolitan yet nearly or factually colonized, central with regard to the non-European margin, yet marginal with regard to the European center. This is, of course, a state which they share not only with each other, but also with any number of similarly ambivalent peripheral European societies. To give but one example, Gregory Jusdanis describes in strikingly cognate terms the "anomalous relationship to Europe" sustained by modern Greece: "It was a European nation yet was located on the periphery of the continent and dominated by the Ottomans for 400 years; Classical Hellas was venerated as the birthplace of civilization whereas modern Greece embarrassed Europeans by its backwardness" (1990, 6). If Greece's compensatory claim to centrality and major status in Europe has derived from its citizens being the descendants of the ancient Greeks, modern Portugal's analogous claim has tended to be based on the country's pioneering role in the Western European enterprise of geographic "discovery" and colonial conquest.

As both Jusdanis and Lloyd, among others, demonstrate, critical approaches to peripheral European cultures have much to gain from the insights afforded by postcolonial perspectives on cultural marginality and hybridization of self and society.[10] However, unexamined adoption of such insights presents various potentially invalidating risks. In the first place, as the editors of the recent *Post-Colonial Studies Reader* argue, referring to "the increasingly unfocused use of the term 'post-colonial' over the last ten years to describe an astonishing variety of cultural, economic and political practices," the tendency to diffuse the designation to characterize any condition of marginality at all "runs the risk of denying its basis in the historical process of [European] colonialism" (Ashcroft, Griffiths, and Tiffin 1995, 2). In addition, and more importantly to the purpose of this argument, while many historically occurring cultural and political phenomena of the European periphery parallel those manifest in the cultures and societies of former European colonies, the paradigms of colonial and postcolonial development offer an analytic tool that is only partially adequate (and, on occasion, patently inadequate) to describing their semiperipheral specificity. For one thing, the historical (as well as metaphorical) colonizer/colonized divide cuts across the varied spectrum of cultures and societies located on the margins of the Northwestern European core, where alongside ex-colonizers, such as Portugal, we find ex-colonies (such as Ireland), as well as any number of nation-states whose historical record makes the rigidity of the distinction entirely problematic. When Eric Hobsbawm calls Portugal at the end of the nineteenth century "a virtual semicolony of Britain" (1987, 18), the awkwardness of the double qualifier points to the difficulties inherent in grafting the lexical and conceptual framework of colonialism onto the European ground.

Furthermore, any analysis of the European periphery's relationship to the continent's political and cultural core must needs take into account the ambivalent nature of that relationship, dialectically suspended between belonging and exclusion. Larry Wolff's richly documented account of the invention of Eastern Europe, by the *philosophes* of the Enlightenment, as a distinct cultural and geopolitical entity that became Western Europe's "complementary other half" (1994, 4), discusses its construction "as a paradox of simultaneous inclusion and exclusion, Europe but not Europe" (7). The attribution of such paradoxical condition has by no means been limited to Eastern Europe—as a well-known dictum would have it, *l'Afrique commence aux Pyrenées*, and travel accounts by French or British visitors to Spain and Portugal are rich in expressions of fascination and bewilderment that would not be out of place in more explicitly extra-European exotic locales. As a result, the notion of "Europe" has figured in the discourses of peripheral autognosis in ways that both approximate and differ markedly from respective colonial and postcolonial articulations, producing a distinct intellectual history of the response to "the imposed images and formulas" devised in the European center, response consisting of "complex cultural strategies of resistance, appropriation, deference, complicity, and counterattack" (Wolff 1994, 373) pursued in the different lands of the European periphery. Moreover, if the dualistic model of the colonial context makes evident "the many ways *nation* and *ethnos* are written as an oppression of 'heathen' Others" (Arteaga 1994, 4; original emphasis), nationalist formulations originating on the European periphery, faced with the paradox of their simultaneous inclusion and exclusion from "Europe," typically negotiate their subject positions as borderline in a tripartite division that accounts for their relation to both the hypercivilized Other of the ultra-European continental core and the uncivilized, "barbarous" Others of the extra-European margin (who may very well claim for themselves a similar borderline identity in their own symbolic topography, pushing the barbaric frontier ever further away from the center).

On the other hand, the inherently and necessarily adversarial stance that postcolonial criticism assumes with regard to the "Eurocentric" perspective does not fully allow for a recognition of the fact that literatures and cultures of the European periphery have only on token occasions been considered as rightful contributors to the common "European" cultural identity. As an anecdotal, but nevertheless highly symptomatic example will show, the affirmation of otherness and marginality—and the consequent verdict of *dispensability*—delivered from the global cultural "core" of Western humanism have been directed not merely at the colonial and postcolonial "barbarians beyond the pale of civilization" (JanMohamed and Lloyd 1990, 2), but also at those semiperipheral cultural formations located at a less categorical distance from the European center.

In 1834, Thomas Babington Macaulay became the president of the Committee on Public Instruction set up eleven years earlier by the British colonial administration in Bengal. As a preliminary step towards producing, the following year, his notorious "Minute on Education," which would lead to the establishment of an educational system aimed at a thorough Anglicization of the East Indian imperial subject, he proffered a supremely arrogant and henceforth much-quoted declaration: "A single shelf of a good European library is worth the whole native literature of India and Arabia" (quoted in B. Anderson 1991, 91). Nearly a century later, an apparently far less arrogant Englishman set out to write a history of Portuguese literature, presenting it as the first systematic endeavor of its kind since the second volume of Friedrich Bouterwek's 1804 *History of Spanish and Portuguese Literature*. It is highly doubtful that Aubrey Bell had Macaulay's dictum on his mind when, in the introductory remarks to what was clearly a labor of long-lasting affection and painstaking erudition, he offered the following merciless judgment of Portuguese literary heritage: "Had one to choose between the loss of the works of Homer, or Dante, or Shakespeare, and that of the whole Portuguese literature, the whole of Portuguese literature must go, but that is not to say that the loss would not be very grievous" (1922, 19). Bell's final softening of the blow notwithstanding (Macaulay would not have bothered), the juxtaposition of the two strikingly similar declarations serves to demonstrate at the very least that the "minority discourses" arising from the European periphery participate in "the common experience of domination and exclusion by the majority" and therefore also share, to a historically variable degree, in "the political and cultural structures that connect different minority cultures in their subjugation and opposition to the dominant culture" (JanMohamed and Lloyd 1990, ix).

In the history of reception and interpretation of the *Lettres portugaises* in Portugal, with its focus on the imagined figure of Soror Mariana Alcoforado as an embodiment of national essence, the semiperipheral anxiety of location emerges as a dominant theme. In fact, it is possible to view the entire process of invention of the Portuguese Nun as an allegorical correlative to cultural negotiation of identity accompanying, particularly since the last decades of the nineteenth century, the gradually unfolding drama of Portuguese geopolitical marginality and semiperipheral ambiguity of status. Is the *alcoforadista* discourse then a "minor" discourse, in the sense proposed by Gilles Deleuze and Félix Guattari and modified, by both Gregory Jusdanis and David Lloyd, for the purposes of their respective analyses of modern Greek culture and Irish literature? Yes and no: their designation of certain discourses as "minor" insists on retaining their oppositional and deconstructive potential vis-a-vis major "myths of identity" (Lloyd 1987, xvii). Lloyd in particular proposes a distinction between "a radically minor literature and one that is still seeking to 'fill a major function'" (1987, 5). Similarly, Jusdanis argues that "minor" should not strive to become "major," but rather derive useful lessons from the condition of its own minority:

> It is not a matter of making the minor "great" but of learning from its prob-
> lematic and of not allowing the "major" and "great" to set the agenda and
> preside over the discussion. . . . From its unique position on the periphery of
> Europe [Greek culture] can play a key role in defamiliarizing the univer-
> salist strategies and global assumptions of traditional scholarship and in
> sensitizing critics to differences among various cultural traditions. (1990, 9)

While this insistence on "the importance of being minor" is very much in agreement with valorization of marginality in postmodern poetics and politics, I would claim that such prescriptive narrowing of the minor con-dition restricts its analytic potential to describe and explain some of the less appealing effects of marginality, in particular those that are contingent precisely on the irrepressible desire to assume or recover a "major func-tion." Deleuze and Guattari have influentially dreamed of "becoming-minor" (1986, 27), but some "minor" dreams can be distinctly unbecoming, corrupted by provincial pettiness and self-perceived irrelevance of their subjects into phantasmagoric nightmares. Moreover, even resolutely "major" discourses of patriotic or chauvinistic affirmation arising from a peripheral location often cannot escape becoming affected, or indeed constituted, by their historically and geopolitically imposed condition of minority. One curious but representative example will help illustrate the predicament I have been describing.

In 1879, a Portuguese scholar, Manuel Bernardes Branco, published a hefty two-volume work, *Portugal e os estrangeiros* [*Portugal and For-eigners*], followed in 1893–95 by three more volumes under the same title. Dedicated to the reigning monarch, Branco's opus was designed, as the author expressed it in his preface, to "prove to the point of evidence that it is glorious to be Portuguese" (v), thus working against the current of social and political criticism fostered by the positivist Geração de 70 (as exemplified by the poet Antero de Quental's famous lecture on the subject of "Causes of the Decadence of the Peninsular Peoples"), not to mention disparaging comments by such occasional foreign observers as, for example, the American Thomas Wentworth Higginson who, in 1856, had diagnosed "Portugal's Glory and Decay." For Branco himself, the need to document his country's "glory" was clearly predicated, if not on explicit admission of its "decay," at least on an unspoken recognition of its undeserved marginality and insignificance on the contemporary world stage. The inaugural claim of his preface presents Portugal as a country which, given its size and geopolitical location, "appeared . . . destined to be forgotten, as its accomplishments would have been unlikely to conquer many pages in history books" (vii). Of course, as Branco's argument goes, the exact opposite happened during the glorious era of the Discoveries: "Portugal, this small, distant corner of the peninsula, emerged from obscurity and forced all the civilized peoples to focus their attention on a single country. . . ." (xi). Further on, the author's narrative oscillates constantly between the antithetic poles of, on the one hand, smallness, marginality, and obscurity, and, on the other, superlative achievement and global projection. What carries his work beyond the commonplace and into the realm of what can only be described as near madness is the dizzying hodgepodge of his references, heaped one upon another in voluminous footnotes that on some pages virtually crowd out the main body of the text. Thus we find out, in rapid and at best tenuously related succession: that a famous eighteenth-century English traveler could speak excellent Portuguese and that on his journey down the Nile he encountered another Englishman who was also proficient in that language; that on an island off the northern coast of Australia the natives appear to know some Portuguese phrases; that an Italian grammarian considers the Portuguese language as rich and harmonious as French or Spanish, and in no way inferior to them; that a Mr. George Harrison from Pennsylvania placed in his garden a statue of the Portuguese poet Filinto Elísio, who had penned an "Ode to American Liberty" (x–xi). Another surreally chaotic catalog enumerates Portuguese natives who had gained celebrity abroad, among them a certain Pereira at the court of Louis XIV, Celestino "the king of Parisian florists," the painter Coelho whose works hang in El Escorial, a professor of Oriental languages in London, a physician in the entourage of Catherine the Great, and a hydraulic engineer from Coimbra who won a prize bestowed by the Royal Academy of Copenhagen. The second installment of Branco's magnum opus, published in the feverish 1890s, after the humiliation of the British Ultimatum had sent the Portuguese society into a collective hysteria, appears even more hectic and disjointed. For instance, the paragraph devoted to a description of the Portuguese community in New Bedford, Massachusetts, closes with a sudden exclamatory comment on the accomplishments of the Portuguese patronage in India; the citation of some casually flattering remarks about Portugal published in an Irish newspaper is absurdly footnoted with an observation about the Portuguese origin of a certain type of irregular garden that became popular in Europe from the sixteenth century onward.

If there is a method to the madness of Branco's collage, its sources must be sought in the overwhelming anxiety of peripheral insignificance leading to the embarrassing exuberance of overcompensation spilling over the top of his catalogs of national achievement. The schizophrenic aspects of his discourse do not, however, point in the direction of deconstructive dismantling of identity: they are symptoms of a desperate yearning for a major status, a pathetically impotent effort to erect a monumental effigy of the marginal nation's irretrievable glory. In addition, *Portugal e os estrangeiros* illustrates, by its very design, what scholars of modern nationalism have widely recognized: the relational nature of the nation's identity, which is construed as much with an eye on what it is (Portugal) as on what it is not (the foreigners). Here, however, "os estrangeiros" do not function merely, or even primarily, as an indispensable element of alterity in the construction of the national self: first and foremost, their role is to validate Portuguese achievement, to elevate it to the major status that it has little hope of attaining otherwise. The mention of a Portuguese traveler in Africa who happened to know English would have no meaning beyond the self-evident; an English explorer proficient in Portuguese is a sign that speaks volumes, as it corroborates the thesis of Portuguese presence on the world stage, of its timeless (if temporarily eclipsed) membership in the permanent cast of globally recognizable political and cultural players.

While in Branco's description Portugal always stands on its own when recognized by a foreigner's privileged and privileging gaze, in actuality it has commonly been perceived as part of the Iberian whole, and a far less important part at that. From the French perspective, as Daniel-Henri Pageaux observes, "the image of Portugal arises always along with the image of Spain, but always in the second place" (1983, 22), as its "double" (24), "pale reflex" or "appendix" (25). For the French writer Montherlant, Portugal appeared as "une femme étendue au flanc d'Espagne" (Pageaux, 25). In his *Histoire politique de l'Europe contemporaine* (1897), Charles Seignobos devoted to Portugal five pages at the end of his chapter on the Iberian Peninsula: in his description of Portuguese civil wars during the first half of the nineteenth century, Seignobos repeated no fewer than eight times the expression "as in Spain." To echo the comment of the Portuguese historian Rui Ramos: " 'As in Spain': such was, at the time, the best summation of nineteenth-century Portuguese history" (1994, 21). Portuguese literature has fared no better. The English translator's preface to the second volume of Friedrich Bouterwek's *History of Spanish and Portuguese Literature* explained how the Portuguese section of the opus had come into being: "M. Bouterwek originally intended to comprise what he had to say, on Portuguese literature, in a brief sketch, which was to form a supplement to the preceding volume; but the assistance of [a learned Portuguese] enabled him to make the present volume a suitable companion to his history of the sister literature of the Peninsula" (1823, 5). It is worth noting here that the writer's anthropomorphic imagination registers a telling slippage: while by virtue of common birth and shared living space, Portuguese literature may be viewed as a "sister" of her Peninsular counterpart, the designation of a "suitable companion" clearly suggests a difference of class status.

If Portugal's "supplementary" status with regard to its Peninsular twin is one constant of its international standing as seen from a European or global point of view, a different picture emerges if we attend instead to the Portuguese perspective. Historically, since at least the late eighteenth century, the chosen European Other of Portuguese cultural elites has been not Spain, but France.[11] For Eduardo Lourenço, the "asymmetric communication" between France and Portugal is a phenomenon of organic proportions:

> As perhaps none other in Europe, Portuguese culture . . . has maintained from its origins a not merely privileged but umbilical relationship with French culture. . . . Having never cut this tie . . . , our culture has accepted and incorporated it down through the centuries, not only in highly diverse terms of dependence or interdependence, but also in ways that were contradictory and even antagonistic. (1983, 16)

Andrée Rocha similarly recognizes "the *constancy* of the fascination that France has held for Portuguese consciousness" (1983, 373; original emphasis), stressing, at the same time, the asymmetric nature of that relationship: "A poor relative in the European family, Portuguese literature has only sporadically managed to cross the Pyrenees" (376). From the other side of the divide, Daniel-Henri Pageaux, as a self-described Lusophile, remorsefully traces the *longues durées* of the relationship that France has over the centuries maintained with Portugal: "These secular tendencies can be named: they are ignorance, indifference, and even contempt" (1983, 12). Ignorance and indifference clearly predominate in his account: for the majority of the French, Portugal remains a "*terra incognita*, an unknown country . . . , a country that has practically no place in French culture" (19).

In the context outlined above, it is no wonder that the story of Soror Mariana Alcoforado and her ill-fated affair with a French aristocrat, followed by a literary triumph of international proportions, should have resonated in multiple ways with Portuguese artists and intellectuals, occasionally rising to the status of an allegorical master fiction reflecting actual and potential relations of Portugal with France and, by a nearly automatic extension, of Portugal with Europe.[12] It is worth noting that the first issue of the Franco-Portuguese journal *Bulletin des Études Portugaises*, published in Coimbra in 1931, which opened with a panoramic overview ("Les Français en Portugal") by Georges Le Gentil, also contained the French translation of Luís Cardim's impassioned defense of Portuguese authenticity of the *Lettres portugaises* (which had originally appeared five years earlier in the journal *A Águia*, as a response to F. C. Green's reopening of the authorship debate). When in 1943 a "Luso-French Cultural Circle of Lower Alentejo" was officially inaugurated in Beja, its president spoke eloquently about "close affinities of heart and spirit" that existed between the town and the French people and evoked Soror Mariana Alcoforado "who passionately gave her whole heart to a Frenchman."[13] Four decades later, the hefty volume of *Les Rapports culturels et littéraires entre le Portugal et la France* (1983), containing selected proceedings of a five-day conference sponsored by the Portuguese Foundation Calouste Gulbenkian, also featured a contribution dedicated to the *Lettres portugaises* (although its French author, Claude-Henri Frèches, bluntly dismissing the discredited hypothesis of a Portuguese original, presented the text as "a French view of Portuguese femininity" [219]). Overall, the rich repository of *alcoforadista* discourse yields a great many examples of the symptomatic relevance of Mariana's love letters, with their diverse interpretations, for the understanding of the historical process of the "asymmetric communication" between the Portuguese periphery and the French or European core. While different aspects of that relationship will be examined in subsequent chapters, it is worth stressing at this point that the underlying emotional structure, which emerges from the assembled body of evidence, is that of an oxymoronic coexistence of xenophilia and xenophobia, a collective *odi et amo* reflecting the discourse of the *Lettres portugaises* themselves in their vacillation between the extremes of absolute, if unrequited, devotion and passionately bitter resentment. Another constant feature, similarly beset by contradiction and saturated with intense emotion, is the compulsion to view the national self through alien (privileged) eyes, typically belonging to a French or British traveler and/or scholar. Luciano Cordeiro, Mariana's preeminent mythographer, writing in the last years of the nineteenth century, shows himself acutely aware of Europe's disdainful gaze upon Portugal. Adopting the French point of view and glossing one seventeenth-century traveler's impressions, he speaks of his Portuguese homeland as "that faraway country where M. de Saint-Romain, in 1665, did not even expect to be able to find kitchen utensils worthy of an envoy of France!" (1888, 49). Cordeiro constantly refers to Soror Mariana as "the poor foreign nun" (1) and, discussing the reception of her letters by the French *salons* of the time, he speaks of an "exotic fruit gathered in a strange and distant land" (6), having already described them, in even more picturesque terms, as "a little anonymous book, which in that gallant, artificial and frivolous setting was . . . like a rough and somber shadow of a monk painted by Zurbaran, falling unexpectedly in the middle of a tender pastoral by Watteau or Boucher" (1).

The preoccupation with what foreigners have thought and written about the country and its people remains current in contemporary Portugal, as Onésimo Teotónio de Almeida points out, citing recent editions of travel writings of William Beckford and Carl Israel Ruders (1991, 493). Lord Byron is perhaps the most vividly remembered among prominent travelers in Portugal, not least for the reflection of his impressions that may be found in the first canto of *Childe Harold's Pilgrimage*. While admiring the landscape, Byron took an exceedingly strong dislike to its native inhabitants, to whom he referred as "Lusian slave[s], the lowest of the low" ("Poor, paltry slaves! yet born 'midst noblest scenes / Why, Nature, waste thy wonders on such men?") (Byron 1980, 17–23). Numerous rebuttals on the part of the justifiably injured "Lusian slaves" have been issued since the poem's publication.[14] A similar reaction of hurt resentment is also clearly detectable in the last major work written in Portugal that engaged in an emotional defense of Soror Mariana's authenticity and her authorship of the letters, *Mariana Alcoforado. A Freira de Beja e as Lettres portugaises* (1966). Its author, António Belard da Fonseca, dedicates a disproportionate amount of attention to a French book by Claude Aveline, published in 1951, which combined an essayistic revisitation of the "case" of the *Lettres portugaises* with a travelogue recounting Aveline's impressions from his trip to Beja. The Frenchman found the town to be distinctly disappointing, immersed in an "unbearable heat" (94) and displaying an incorrect sort of exotic images ("peasants on horseback . . . imitated William Hart and Rio Jim's films, and transformed our desert into the pampas or the American West!" [61]). While appreciating Aveline's interest in Mariana and his faith in the authenticity of her letters, Fonseca chides him for his misrepresentation of Beja: the town's streets cannot be described as "dusty," since they are paved with cobblestones or covered with asphalt; it is impossible for the mattress on Aveline's hotel bed to have been filled with seaweed, since it is not used in Alentejo; as for the noisy army barracks across the street from the hotel, they have already been moved to a new building on the outskirts of the town (123–25). Besides, Fonseca points out, Parisian hotels are often no better than those in Beja: he himself, on his trips to the French capital, had to suffer "constant nightly noise of delivery trucks on their way to the Halles" (125), among other indignities.

The degree of importance ascribed by these and other Portuguese authors to external images of the national culture, along with the powerful emotional charge which has historically tended to accompany their reception and interpretation, point to the concept of collective space that the anthropologist Michael Herzfeld describes as "cultural intimacy" (1997, x). Cultural intimacy flourishes in "the privacy of nations" (x), as a "defensive domesticity" (4), and its most telltale signs are "those aspects of a cultural identity that are considered a source of external embarrassment but that nevertheless provide insiders with their assurance of common sociality" (3). The resulting duality of national self-images is also analyzed by Herzfeld under the rubric of "*disemia*—the formal or coded tension between official self-presentation and what goes on in the privacy of collective introspection" (14; original emphasis). Disemic shifts, gaps, and crossings between the images of national culture produced for external use—"*para o inglês ver*," for the Englishman to see, as a common Portuguese saying has it—and the deeply rooted, at the same time collective and private, national self-awareness, will be frequently addressed in the following pages. In fact, it could hardly be otherwise: the external and the internal perspectives are inseparably intertwined in the "reexported," Franco-Portuguese fiction of Soror Mariana.

As Herzfeld also recognizes, the discerning gaze of the external "specialist"—an anthropologist, a historian, a cultural critic—is very much part of the equation of cultural intimacy. In fact, it was through an analysis of his own interactions with his Greek research subjects over the years that the design of his study emerged, prompted by Herzfeld's "increasing fascination with the desire for control over the external images of a national culture" expressed in denials, prohibitions, and evasive actions directed against the curious outsider (ix). I have also experienced such curiosity and fascination—and such awareness of an intimate national space to which I had at best a limited access—during the past twenty years of my apprenticeship of Portuguese culture. At the same time, I have always remained on the outside looking in, unlike some other foreign observers who chose to develop strong personal ties to the land and its people before claiming any degree of authority to be able to proclaim themselves on its matters (incidentally, Portugal has had a long-standing tradition of welcoming and cherishing such naturalized external participants in its intellectual and artistic life). If, in spite of this limitation, I have chosen to trespass on this difficult ground, at times a veritable minefield, it is partly because I can claim a native familiarity with a culture whose peripheral European location has made it a similarly fertile ground for many of the cultural, social, and psychological phenomena that were also instrumental in the invention of the Portuguese Nun as a national myth and, more generally, in determining certain specific traits of Portuguese cultural reality. In particular the Poland in which I grew up, separated as it was from "Europe" by the Iron Curtain, cultivated almost obsessively its semiperipheral anxiety (and on occasion, paranoia), its schizophrenic conjunction of the complexes of inferiority and superiority, and its love-hate relationships with the outside world.

More important, however, for the purposes of this particular story, than my inbred competence in detecting symptoms of certain national pathologies, is the fact that I have come to live and work in between geocultural sites and in between national languages, without any essentialized cultural or national location to claim as fully my own, much as that incarnation of the elusive "Mariana" of the *Lettres portugaises* that I am about to add to the repository of her fame. As the Three Marias wrote over twenty-five years ago, "What sort of metaphor is Mariana for us if we almost kill ourselves in order to leave her out?" (35).

2

Inventing Mariana

WHEN IN DECEMBER 1823 AN ARISTOCRATIC PORTUGUESE EXPATRIATE, José Maria de Sousa Botelho (Morgado de Mateus), signed his initials to an erudite *notice bibliographique* that was to serve as a preface to a new edition of the *Lettres portugaises*, he was keenly aware of his pioneering role in what he saw as a necessary enterprise of national reappropriation of this epistolary masterpiece. He recalled his youthful enthusiasm at first having read the letters at the age of eighteen, as well as his amazement that no national claim to their authorship had ever been laid before: "I was surprised that, so many years after their publication, no Portuguese had ever tried to put them back into our own language, and thus lay claim to a part of our national patrimony" (34).

Although Sousa Botelho had then proceeded immediately to produce his own translation of the letters into Portuguese, he hesitated for many years to publish his work, hoping that a more able translator might dedicate himself to the task. In the end he decided to overcome his reluctance: "I am therefore daring to publish [the translation] across from the text, so that readers, perceiving its difficulty, might excuse me. Let them consider that for over a century no Portuguese has ever tried to reclaim this national treasure" (38).

Sousa Botelho seemed unaware that some years earlier another expatriate writer, also based in Paris, had in fact both translated and published a Portuguese version of the *Lettres*. However, that pioneering translation, by the neoclassical poet Francisco Manuel do Nascimento, known by his Arcadian name of Filinto Elísio, appeared tucked away modestly in the tenth volume of the author's collected works published for the first time in the year of his death at the ripe age of eighty-four (*Obras completas*. Paris: A. Bobbe, 1819). Accompanied by no introductory remarks or commentary, the translation was thus unlikely to attract much immediate attention.

All the same, there was a distinctly apposite logic to Filinto Elísio's interest in returning the *Lettres portugaises* to their presumed original idiom. In
what is arguably his most important work, written also in his old age and
in the deepening isolation and destitution of his Parisian existence, the
poet issued a proud and spirited defense of his native language's classical
virtues. His epistle in verse entitled "Da Arte Poética Portuguesa" criti-
cized severely the writer's contemporaries for allowing the Portuguese
idiom to be contaminated by the influence of "bastard Gallicisms," rather
than looking to Latin for a legitimate source of linguistic rejuvenation and
improvement: "Never a French nose on the Lusian face, / Who is an offspring of Latin" (1836–40, 119). French intellectuals professing their admiration for Camões were also chastised for reading the sixteenth-century
poet in the "insipid prose" of the French translation, instead of taking the
trouble of learning Portuguese in order to be able to appreciate the text in
its original greatness. Against this overwhelming deluge of Frenchifica-
tion, the old poet's resolve to translate the *Lettres portugaises* into Portuguese emerges as a subversively contrarian move and an apt point of
departure for the entire history of their adoption as a national masterpiece
of Portugal.

Following the labors of the two expatriates, it is possible to detect a
gradually increasing awareness of the existence and potential significance
of the *Lettres portugaises* for Portuguese national culture. It was, at first, a
very slow trickle: as late as 1847, José Silvestre Ribeiro, the author of a
book portraying *Beja no anno de 1845*, did not list Mariana Alcoforado
among "Naturaes de Beja Grandes em Letras" (31–37) and his omission
(which a few decades later would stand out as glaring) appeared to be
caused by sheer ignorance rather than by a conscious, morally correct act
of censorship against a wayward nun, a putative attitude some writers
would later blame for Beja's long-lasting neglect of the town's most
famous inhabitant. Indeed, Ribeiro's lack of recognition of Mariana Alcoforado's international fame may be explained by the fact that, as the
author himself states, his main bibliographic source for the respective
chapter was Diogo Barbosa Machado's *Bibliotheca lusitana* (1741–59),
which had been published much too early to contain a mention of the Portuguese Nun. By 1862, Inocêncio Francisco da Silva, when compiling the
respective installment of his monumental, multivolume *Dicionário Bibli-
ográfico Português* (later to be known simply as "Inocêncio"), registered
a mention of the *Lettres portugaises*, but chose to withhold judgment as to
their national authenticity. A few years later, in his *Curso de Literatura
Portuguesa* (1876), Camilo Castelo Branco was adamant in his exclusion

of the nun's letters from Portuguese literary heritage and approvingly cited Jean Jacques Rousseau's famous dictum regarding the impossibility of female authorship.[1] It is important to note, however, that, skeptical as he was of the letters' authenticity, Camilo no longer felt it possible to leave out any mention of them from his panoramic overview of seventeenth-century Portuguese literary production, thus confirming their prominent presence in the ongoing formation of the national canon (see chapter 4: Canonizing Mariana, for a full account of this process).[2]

While in the Portuguese controversy over the authenticity of the *Lettres portugaises* polemic interventions from the anti-*alcoforadista* faction (pioneered by Camilo) tended to be provoked by various militant and rhetorically exuberant affirmations penned by proponents and defenders of Soror Mariana's fame (with Teófilo Braga as an early but nearly unsurpassed master of the art of mythmaking apotheosis), the *alcoforadistas* themselves were often spurred to action by occasional reports and statements on the question issuing from France, dispatches as avidly received as they were infrequent. In one of the first such cases, occurred in 1885, a researcher from the town of Beaune in Burgundy, E. Beauvois, published in the archives of the local historical society (and reprinted in book form) a biographic study of the Maréchal de Chamilly, with a polemic chapter dedicated to the *Lettres portugaises*. Adamantly opposed to the tradition that had long attributed to Chamilly the role of the Portuguese Nun's faithless lover, and describing the letters as a poorly executed fake, Beauvois waged battle for a "complete rehabilitation" (355) of his locally prominent subject and in the process hurled some rather gratuitous insults at the fictitious heroine whom he called a madwoman, a fury, and an obsessed Maenad (363–64).

It did not take long for a compatriot of thus besmirched Soror Mariana to come to her defense. In 1888, Luciano Cordeiro published what was destined to become a definitive statement and a perennial classic of Portuguese *alcoforadista* literature. Cordeiro's *Soror Mariana, a freira portuguesa* was, however, more than a rhetorically impassioned retort to Beauvois or another factually unfounded statement on behalf of the authenticity of the *Lettres portugaises* and their national legitimacy. Based on extensive research conducted by the author in the archives of Beja, the book presented a considerable amount of previously unpublished evidence. Cordeiro was able to prove that Mariana Alcoforado had in fact existed, had been a nun in the Convento da Conceição, and was about twenty-five years old at the time of Chamilly's sojourn in Portugal; he unearthed records of her baptism in 1640, as well as her death certificate

dating from 1723, along with other documents corroborating the historical Mariana's identity. These proofs, ingeniously woven together with a
comprehensive amount of background information drawn from various
seventeenth-century conventual sources, formed the core of what a later
critic would call Cordeiro's "work of exuberant imagination . . . a house
of cards with the arrogance of a skyscraper" (Rodrigues 1935, 93). For
while the mysterious handwritten note, revealed in 1810 by Boissonade,
in which the name of "Mariana Alcaforada" had for the first time been
brought to light, became now much more difficult to dismiss as one fan-
ciful reader's groundless speculation, Cordeiro's contribution did nothing
to establish any sort of evidence of personal contact that may have occurred between the nun and the chevalier, much less prove Mariana's authorship of the famous love letters.

Just who was Luciano Cordeiro? A onetime fellow traveler of the positivist Geração de 70, who actually contributed a pamphlet of his own to
the contentious *Questão coimbrã*, in later years Cordeiro displayed considerable versatility as a public figure. Having at first considered a military career in the navy, he went on to study literature, as well as economy
and political science. For several years he held a teaching post at the
Royal Military College and also lectured at other institutions of higher
learning. He contributed to and served on editorial boards of a number of
periodicals, eventually directing a newspaper of his own, Lisbon's *Jornal
da Noite*. He helped found the Geographical Society of Lisbon (1876) and
was awarded the position of its permanent secretary. As a career bureau-
crat, he directed a number of organs of Portuguese civil administration.
The extensive list of Cordeiro's publications imparts a similarly kaleido-
scopic impression, not uncharacteristic, it needs to be stressed, of a
nineteenth-century Portuguese intellectual.[3] His first major book was a
collection of essays of literary and art criticism (*Livro de crítica. Arte e
literatura portuguesa de hoje, 1868-1869*, published in 1869); the following more or less random selection of additional titles illustrates the far-
flung scope of the author's concerns (as well as, less charitably put, his
likely propensity toward educated dilettantism): *Da literatura como
revelação social* (1872); *O casamento dos padres* (1872); *Portugal e o
Movimento Geográfico Moderno* (1877); *Estudos bancários* (1877); *A
hidrografia africana no século XVI* (1878); *Portugueses fora de Portugal.
Uma sobrinha do Infante Imperatriz da Alemanha e Rainha da Hungria*
(1894).

Notwithstanding the prolific versatility of Cordeiro's interests, in the
years immediately preceding the publication of *Soror Mariana* one area in

particular virtually monopolized his intellectual and political activity. That area was the very current *questão colonial*, which had gained renewed momentum since the 1870s, as European countries escalated and intensified their competition for the redistribution of extra-European colonial wealth. Largely as a result of that process, with its most dramatic manifestation in the so-called "Scramble for Africa," the last decades of the nineteenth century witnessed, as well, a traumatic redefinition of Portugal's geopolitical status in Europe and in the world. That status could be described as highly "anomalous," an adjective employed by David Lloyd to describe Ireland's "anomalous position as at once a European nation and a colony" (1987, ix). Portugal's position in the new world order being forged at the close of the nineteenth century appeared as even more contradictory: the country was at the same time the metropolis of a still vast colonial empire and a poor relative among European nation-states, described by Eric Hobsbawm as "small, feeble, backward" and "a virtual semi-colony of England" (1987, 18). As Hobsbawm also notes, "the survival of the major Portuguese territories in Africa . . .was due primarily to the inability of their modern rivals to agree on the exact manner of dividing them among themselves" (57). In fact, the right of Portugal to retain its colonial possessions was being openly disputed: in the spirit of the Darwinian-Spenserian "survival of the fittest," at the time gaining currency in international politics, British, German, and French diplomats often discussed the appropriateness of leaving the authority over such vast territories in the hands of a state as destitute as Portugal. Portugal's mightier peninsular neighbor, even while heading toward a global crisis of its own, was inclined to join the majority vote on the issue: in an 1889 lecture, the Spanish writer Rafael Labra could argue that Portugal was much too poor for its colonial claims (Ramos 1994, 32).

As Nuno Severiano Teixeira notes, the political and economic enterprise of slicing up those areas of the world that European jurists referred to as *res nullius* was accompanied by the forging of great imperial ideologies, organized around materially concrete core concepts such as Cecil Rhodes' trajectory "from Cape to Cairo," but governed in nearly all the cases by a transcendental sense of a "historical mission" or "national destiny" (1987, 689). As Teixeira continues,

> The Portuguese case seems exemplary in this respect. A complex blend of political and economic reasons, the Portuguese colonial project has historically claimed the mantle of a "national mission." The notion of Portugal's "colonial vocation" extends from the ideologues of the Geographical Society

. . . through Gilberto Freyre's Luso-Tropicalism, all the way to the theories of Marcelo Caetano. (689)

As the founding member and permanent secretary of the Geographic Society, Cordeiro played a prominent role in the ideological enterprise of justifying and defending Portuguese interests overseas, particularly in Africa.[4] Those interests, traditionally buttressed by the principle of historic rights (with reference to Portugal's pioneering role in the history of European expansion and colonization), from the mid-1870s found themselves challenged by arguments giving primacy to the principle of effective occupation, a ground on which Portugal could not hope to compete with its more powerful European counterparts (Teixeira 1987, 690). In 1884, Cordeiro was a member of the Portuguese delegation at the international Berlin Conference, a major turning point in the colonial history of the world, where effective occupation was conclusively affirmed as the guiding principle of European jurisdiction overseas. The dramatic tone of his writing at the time testifies to Portugal's beleaguered standing on the international scene:

> What will be the fate of our African possessions, our colonial sovereignty, our overseas trade, what shall become of our name, our traditions, our hopes, our vast interests in Africa, if another nation, if other nations . . . manage to open wide, without us and against us, that enormous and opulent continent, which we, centuries ago, discovered, conquered, and evangelized . . . ? (Cordeiro 1981, 23).

It was amidst such a climate that Cordeiro conceived of and carried out the substantial labor of researching and writing his *Soror Mariana*. Far from an escapist endeavor, his initiative was part and parcel of a massive and multifaceted cultural campaign, whose starting point may be seen in the exuberant celebrations of the tricentennial of Luís de Camões that took place in 1880. In a series of articles published in *Comércio de Portugal* in January 1880, Teófilo Braga promoted the idea of the tricentennial as a "ceremony of national consecration," noting that, similarly to Cervantes in Spain, Voltaire in France, Dante, Petrarch, and Michelangelo in Italy, Camões represented "the synthesis of the national character" of Portugal (Santos 1932, 286). The Geographic Society and Luciano Cordeiro played a prominent role in organizing and carrying out the celebrations, hosting many preparatory meetings and related cultural events. As F. Reis Santos wrote in his contribution to the monumental history of the Republican movement in Portugal organized by Luís de Montalvor (1932),

The tricentennial celebrations brought to life, for the first time in modern Portugal, a nation that was disunited, unconscious of itself and completely divorced from its great traditions. The festivities awoke, by way of Camões the brilliant singer of the nation's feats, Portugal's feeling for its shining and heroic past. (262)

Following the Camões celebrations, many similar initiatives took place, allowing Reis Santos to characterize the period between 1880 and 1891 as the time when modern Portugal "felt . . . for the first time the sad contrast between its brilliant and glorious past and its dull and precarious present" (261). This imperative desire to revive the nation's ancient glories, coupled with humiliating awareness of Portugal's cultural, as well as geopolitical, insignificance on the European stage, similarly informed the design of Cordeiro's study of Soror Mariana. Prompted by disdainful remarks of a provincial French historian, it sought to complete the necessary task of restoring the *Lettres portugaises*, along with their unfortunate and maligned author, to their rightful place in the Portuguese cultural heritage.

It may be worth noting here that the embattled rhetoric of a peripheral culture, alternatively ignored or derided, attempting to assert itself against the European political and cultural center, had long been present in Cordeiro's writing. In an early polemical brochure, he denounced the negative image of Portugal propagated by foreigners, particularly by the British:

For years, any *quidam* of the United Kingdom who might have spent a few months among us . . . considered himself . . . possessed of an unalienable right or an exacting duty to write . . . an intense diatribe against our sanctimonious habits, our inquisitorial fanaticism, and finally against our uncommon ignorance, indolence, cowardice and other such traits that have combined to fashion us, in the eyes of Europe, into a nation of barbarians.

Many a time it would turn out that the illustrious author . . . had never been to Portugal and did not even know whether Portugal was some Polynesian island or a kingdom of Europe. (1865, 37–38)

Cordeiro's introductory remarks to *Soror Mariana* likewise set the culturally adversarial tone that continued to echo repeatedly throughout his work. Mariana Alcoforado was a "poor foreign nun" (1888, 1) whose heartfelt, yearning letters contrasted jarringly with detached, sophisticated stylistics of seventeenth-century French amorous discourse. Her country was, for the French, a remote outpost of their cultural empire, "something akin . . . to what other peoples represented to a citizen of ancient Rome"

(7). Similarly unequal destiny befell the Portuguese nun and the French chevalier after their love affair had run its course: "For thirty years did the wretched seduced nun of Beja . . . torment her soul and her body in the mystical idiocy of her cloistered penitence, while her illustrious seducer marched gloriously through life, covered with fame and fat" (84). In short, the *Lettres portugaises* became, in Cordeiro's fertile imagination, *portuguesas* in a sense deeper and more complex than a simple skirmish over literary attribution might imply: their origin and history were shaped into an allegorical representation of Portugal's peripheral predicament in Europe and in the world, a predicament whose long tradition was being dramatically mirrored and exacerbated by the events of the late nineteenth century.

The concept of national allegory has most commonly been discussed with regard to the literary genre of the novel, particularly in relationship to what Doris Sommer has termed the "foundational fictions" produced in newly emergent nations of nineteenth-century Latin America, whose coherence derived from "their common need to reconcile and amalgamate national constituencies, and from the strategy to cast the previously unreconciled parties, races, classes, or regions, as lovers who are 'naturally' attracted and right for one another" (1990, 81). By contrast, the allegorical potential carried by the story of Soror Mariana Alcoforado became evident and attractive to Portuguese intellectuals, such as Cordeiro, because of its ability to represent a nation in crisis perceived to have been caused by external forces, as a drama of betrayal and abandonment. Mariana's predicament—as female, provincial, leading a cloistered and uninspiring existence, abandoned by a dashing French lover, and longing helplessly for the absent man and his faraway country, even while also asserting her pride and independence—resonated in multiple and often contradictory ways with writers and historians attempting to come to terms with progressive marginalization of Portugal with regard to major European colonial powers, most notably France and England.

Allegorical retellings of the story of Mariana Alcoforado in Portugal once again help bring into focus the issue of applicability of postcolonial analysis to political and cultural realities of the European periphery. As Fredrick Jameson has powerfully if also controversially argued, national allegory may be considered a dominant mode of cultural production in third-world societies: "Third-world texts, even those which are seemingly private and invested with a properly libidinal dynamic—necessarily project a political dimension in the form of national allegory: *the story of the private individual destiny is always an allegory of the embattled situation of the public third-world culture and society*" (1986, 69; original emphasis). Whereas in Western European tradition it is political commitment that becomes "recontained and psychologized or subjectivized" in cultural production, in third-world texts, by contrast, this relation is inverted and, as Jameson proposes, "psychology, or more specifically, libidinal investment, is to be read in primarily political and social terms" (71–72). Although Jameson's essay for the most part relies on a rigid and, as Aijaz Ahmad points out in his critique, empirically ungrounded "binary opposition . . . between a capitalist first world and a presumably pre- or non-capitalist third world" (1987, 7), the critic does acknowledge, if only for the purposes of exclusionary narrowing of his discussion, the existence of other, categorically distinct, world spaces: the socialist "second world" (which, writing from his relatively stable and by now irreparably dated vantage point of the mid-1980s, he can still afford to bypass in his analysis); and, more importantly here, the general space of the European periphery. The test case is provided by the nineteenth-century Spanish novels of Benito Pérez Galdós, specifically his masterpiece *Fortunata y Jacinta* (1887). While Jameson detects in the novel's plot the same structure of politically and nationally specific allegorical reference that he has deemed characteristic of third-world texts, he chooses to stress what he calls its "optional nature": "we can use it to convert the entire situation of the novel into an allegorical commentary on the destiny of Spain, but we are also free to reverse its priorities and to read the political analogy as metaphorical decoration for the individual drama, and as a mere figural intensification of this last" (78–79). The notion of ambiguous "reversibility," which according to Jameson characterizes allegoric interpretation performed in semiperipheral locations, is a compelling one, a yet another manifestation of the ambivalently "anomalous" nature of cultural and political formations of the European margin.[5]

The story of the Portuguese Nun, as told in an allegorical mode by Luciano Cordeiro, proved to be a convincing and influential one. The publication of *Soror Mariana, a freira portuguesa* snowballed into a cultural event of considerable proportions, ably stimulated by promotional initiatives undertaken by the author and his publisher, Livraria Ferin. Advance copies were sent to all major newspapers as well as to a number of prominent individuals (among them the historian Oliveira Martins), and Cordeiro's own *Jornal da Noite* assiduously reprinted comments from the press spilling over its pages in an "enthusiastic and uncontrollable deluge of grandiloquent prose" (Rodrigues 1935, 93).[6] On Sunday, 19 August 1888, the day before the book was to be released, Lisbon's *Repórter* assured its readers that *Soror Mariana* would be a certain success, and several other advance notices followed suit. The first comprehensive review appeared three days later in Porto's *Jornal de Notícias*, which stressed the patriotic dimension of Cordeiro's work:

> The illustrious writer Luciano Cordeiro has rendered a most valuable service to national literature. . . . The distinguished writer's new book . . . represents, in addition to its great merit as a work of literature, an important service to the good name of the country. (reprinted in *Jornal da Noite*, 22 August 1888)

Writing in *Esquerda Dinástica*, António Campos Júnior struck a similar chord, praising in Cordeiro "the tireless combatant, glorious excavator of old geographic matters, . . . brilliant reconqueror of many [national] glories flaunted by foreign perfidy," and concluding that "*Soror Mariana* is among Luciano Cordeiro's most valuable books" (*Jornal da Noite*, 30 August 1888). Mariana's original champion, Teófilo Braga, published an enthusiastic review in *Democracia*, recognizing in Cordeiro's work "a superb national repossession" and bestowing upon the author "the glory of restituting irreversibly this resplendent page to the history of our seventeenth century and this everlasting monument to the Portuguese nation" (*Jornal da Noite*, 3 September 1888). Several reviewers echoed Cordeiro's rhetorical strategy in drawing an antithetical distinction between French and Portuguese national characters; however, a review of *Soror Mariana* written by Mme Adam, the editor of the Parisian *Nouvelle Revue*, was given first-page prominence when it was reprinted, in its original French, in the *Jornal da Noite*. Ironically, Mme Adam's review struck an already familiar sympathetic chord, lamenting the fact that "the language of Camoens is so little known in France," and therefore that Cordeiro's study would have fewer readers there than it deserved to attract (*Jornal da Noite*, 30 October 1888). Other authors took advantage of the publishing event to foster cultural and political agendas of their own. Thus, *Folha do Povo*'s reviewer sounded an anticlerical and antimonastic note, noting that Cordeiro, in addition to rendering "a relevant service to national letters, contributed a tremendous weapon to the struggle against the black vultures who divert woman from the family in order to bury her in the sterile suffering of the cloister" (*Jornal da Noite*, 22 August 1888). Writing in *Ilustração*, a Portuguese periodical published in Paris, Mariano Pina engaged in a long diatribe against the quality of public secondary education in Portugal. Confessing to feelings of shame he endured when comparing himself to "any French youth with a baccalaureate in the humanities," he went on to vilify the Portuguese educational establishment in the strongest terms, pointing to it as "the reason for our anarchy, ignorance and intellectual misery" (*Jornal da Noite*, 7 November 1888).

It is worth noting at this juncture that while reviews of Cordeiro's *Soror Mariana* provided their authors with a convenient forum to air their deep-seated grievances about Portuguese marginality and inferiority, particularly with regard to France, they were hardly the only journalistic interventions published at the time that addressed the issue. On 22 September 1888, a front-page correspondence from France published in *Jornal da Noite* related an embarrassing incident at the Portuguese consulate in Paris and went on to comment on the identity of Portugal, seen through implicit French eyes as "*un pays lointain*—a land out of a legend, lost on the margins of history and of the world, an entity more fantastic than the republic of Andorra."

Soon enough, however, all these multiple concerns occupying Portuguese intellectual elites would become overshadowed by, or rather subsumed in, what has been described as the most acute political crisis of burgeoning Portuguese modernity, the case of the so-called British Ultimatum. On 11 January 1890, England's prime minister, Lord Salisbury, addressed a brief memorandum to the Portuguese government. The document stated that unless Portugal withdrew her armed forces from an area to the west of northern Mozambique, England would consider breaking the ancient Anglo-Portuguese Alliance and dispatching naval units to Mozambique and possibly to Portugal itself (Wheeler 1993, 175). Her Majesty's ship *Enchantress* was stationed in Vigo, just north of the Portuguese border with Spain, awaiting orders from the British minister in Lisbon, who had been instructed to leave Portugal at once with all the members of his legation unless he was given an immediate satisfactory answer to England's demands (Coelho 1990, 173). The Portuguese government had no other choice than to submit to the ultimatum, causing an unprecedented outpouring of public agitation, in which Cordeiro and the Geographic Society played a highly prominent role. The Lisbon newspaper *Tempo* reported the following incident in its edition of 13 January:

From Serpa Pinto Street, the demonstrators made their way to Capello Street, coming to a stop in front of the Geographic Society where the [national] flag had been brought half way down the pole. There the crowd once again shouted "Long live Portugal" and "Down with England." Mr. Luciano Cordeiro . . . appeared in one of the windows and spoke with great passion, receiving extraordinary applause. His every word was followed by thunderous clapping and prolonged cheering.

Among all the public associations in Portugal that made their contribution to the massive campaign of protest, from the Agricultural League of Beja (which declared it would no longer purchase any English-made tools or products) to the Zoological Garden of Lisbon (which offered a portion of its receipts to support a national subscription), the Geographic Society, with Cordeiro at its helm, was by far the most actively and consistently involved in the outpouring of remonstrations against the Ultimatum (Teixeira 1987, 706–8). In addition, Cordeiro's *Jornal da Noite*, along with the rest of Portuguese Republican press, remained absorbed in spinning out political commentary that combined nationalist and anti-British arguments with pro-Republican and antimonarchic propaganda. As Maria Teresa Pinto Coelho notes, the inflation of the Ultimatum episode into a national trauma of unprecedented dimensions can to a large extent be attributed to the inflammatory rhetoric of the Republican press: "The Republicans spread the image of Portugal as a country in decay and seized the opportunity to proclaim themselves the redeemers of the Portuguese nation" (1990, 183). The crisis brought thus into relief an alliance of external and internal factors in Portuguese politics and culture at the end of the nineteenth century: Portugal's increasingly evident marginalization on the international scene became intertwined with Republican propaganda, which seized upon the humiliation of the Ultimatum in order to blame the monarchy for the "decadence" into which the country had fallen (Teixeira 1987, 718).

If, a little over a year before the crisis of the Ultimatum erupted, Júlio César Machado had been able to refer to 1888 as "The Year of the Nun" in his enthusiastic review of Cordeiro's *Soror Mariana* (*Jornal da Noite*, 19 September 1888), soon enough there was no doubt in anyone's mind that 1890 would forever be remembered in Portugal as the year of the British Ultimatum.[7] Nevertheless, Luciano Cordeiro was able to combine his intense involvement in the political events of the crisis with preparation of a second, expanded edition of his acclaimed study of the Portuguese Nun. Generously supplemented by illustrations, some featuring documents newly unearthed by the author, the book was put on sale in January 1891. Clearly capitalizing on the success of the first edition, Livraria Ferin this time produced a far more handsome volume, printed on expensive paper and adorned with a portrait of the author in the frontispiece. In their introductory note, the publishers bragged of the extraordinary success enjoyed by the book, which had sold out in two months' time during the summer and early fall, "precisely the months known as the worst on our book selling market" (Cordeiro 1891, 7). They also remarked on the many requests for a second edition that had been received by the house and noted that a considerable number of those had arrived from foreign countries (9).

It is worth remarking at this point that the enthusiastic reception enjoyed by Cordeiro's *Soror Mariana* was to a considerable degree driven by the book's press coverage, which, aside from being uniformly favorable, pointed to an overarching significance of the author's goals and methods in his contemporary Portuguese context. In short, the book was received as a distinctly modern response to the demands of the country's literate middle-class population. As José Tengarrinha comments in his analysis of the transformations undergone by the Portuguese and European press in the years 1865–85, newspaper readers had begun to show a marked preference "for *objective information* (as opposed to *opinion*), as well as for a *sensationalist* bent that its presentation gradually acquired," an attitude which the author explains by referring to "a new *mentality* of the petty and middle bourgeoisie affected by the serious ideological crisis of the last quarter of the century" (1988, 193; original emphasis). The readers' predilection for sensational items was to influence, on the one hand, the nature and content of the news deemed fit and desirable to print (hence, for example, reporting of gruesome crimes became a reliable staple); on the other hand, it led to spectacular popularity enjoyed by the feuilleton, a regular section of the newspaper devoted to light fiction, reviews, and articles aimed at general entertainment. It is instructive to note that most of the critical appreciations of *Soror Mariana* that appeared in various Portuguese publications and were reprinted in Cordeiro's *Jornal da Noite* in the fall of 1888 found their typesetting niche precisely in the space of that newspaper's feuilleton, at first preempting, then alternating with, its current serialization of Alexandre Dumas's novel *Les louves de Machecoul*. What's more, while fictional narratives of adventures or love stories offered the newspaper-reading public a much desired "emotional escape from the boredom of daily routine" (Tengarrinha, 193), Cordeiro's study of the Portuguese Nun satisfied, in a uniquely symbiotic manner, the often contradictory demands of scientific objectivity and novelistic sensationalism. As Guiomar Torresão wrote in *A Ilustração Portuguesa* (17 September 1888),

In Luciano Cordeiro's book, the figure of Mariana Alcoforado, the Lusitanian Heloise, has for the first time emerged from dark obscurity in which she
lay enveloped and has become revealed in all her strange beauty, adorned
with fabulous trappings of a legend, but made alive by a sudden flash of log-
ically reasoned critical illumination. (4)

Moreover, as several reviewers were eager to point out, this "logical"
and "critical" objectivity of *Soror Mariana* constituted yet another important angle of the book's national significance. Pinheiro Chagas argued that
Cordeiro had learned to proceed methodically and scientifically in his historical investigations through his frequent dealings with European scholars
and politicians, whose influence made him wary of "temptations of national superficiality" prevalent in the Portuguese context (*A Ilustração
Portuguesa*, 22 October 1888): "When he had to debate African matters
with German scholars in Berlin, he saw that it was necessary to probe
deeply in order to combat against such heavy adversaries, whose ranks are
not likely to be broken by the light cavalry of our experts."

In other words, it was only through the production of cultural artifacts
such as Cordeiro's *Soror Mariana* (and of political artifacts such as his arguments on behalf of Portuguese rights in Africa), which couched their
postulates of national revindication in terms sufficiently objective and
rigorous to match the criteria of scientific legitimacy prevailing in the
European core, that the peripheral Portugal could hope to cast off its
stigma of inferiority and decadence.

However, notwithstanding their rhetorical privileging of "scientific" objectivity, virtually all the writings, by Cordeiro and others, that compose
the canon of *alcoforadista* gospel have situated themselves, by necessity,
in the vast space of cultural invention "between truth and history . . .
[space] occupied by constructed images, often as or more effective than
what has 'really happened' " (Buescu 1991, 50). Two major areas where
the invention of Soror Mariana, as the author of the *Lettres portugaises*
and a representative figure of national culture, has taken place are territorial siting and familial genealogy. As Perry Anderson points out, all ethnic
mythologies "are either territorial or genealogical in character—tracing
the identity of the group to an original location or a primordial ancestry"
(1991, 5). Although Anderson posits those "basic mythemes" at the origin
of more elaborate constructs of space and memory found in later nationalist ideologies, it should be observed that there exists no record of either
"territorial" or "genealogical" mythology of Mariana Alcoforado in Portugal prior to the nationalistic appropriation of her story in the nineteenth

century. Only throughout the process and in the aftermath of that enterprise of cultural invention did the figure of the Portuguese Nun become
grafted onto the regional soil of Beja and the Alentejo, as well as, secon-
darily, into the familial narrative of the Alcoforados.

If, at the turn of the century, Portugal appeared as peripheral and inferior
on the European scene, Beja, the main municipality of Lower Alentejo,
was among Portugal's own most severely marginalized internal periph-
eries. To cite just one culturally significant aspect of its underdevelopment,
of the 416 periodical publications published throughout the country in
1900, only two appeared in Beja, with a total of 1,300 weekly copies.
Given that the literacy rate among the town's male population (no data
exists for females) was at the time 23 percent, periodical readership reveals a staggering ratio of fourteen potential readers per one circulating
copy (compared to three readers per copy in the northern city of Braga,
which in many other respects was equally provincial) (Ramos 1994, 48).
As Rui Ramos comments, what these data mean is that Beja "could have at
least five times more periodical copies in circulation if its literate inhabitants were as interested in reading as those of Braga, or if Beja had a publishing tradition comparable to that apparently existing in the northern
district" (48).

It is hardly surprising, therefore, that comments on the story of the Portuguese Nun emanating from the metropolitan centers of Lisbon and Porto
would emphasize the remoteness and exoticism of her monastic abode,
curiously echoing the tone of remarks by French or British readers with
regard to the exotic marginality of Portugal. In his review of Cordeiro's
book, one writer spoke of Mariana's life in "a convent lost in the solitary
reaches of Alentejo" and many others would sound a similar note.[8] It was
as if the national "discovery" of the prodigious nun of Beja had opened up
to the geographical and cultural elites of Portugal's major cities an internal, hidden periphery, clouded by its obscurity and insignificance, but for
that very reason irresistibly appealing as a fitting backdrop for Mariana's
passionate narrative of yearning and abandonment. The Alentejan origin of
the *Lettres portugaises* became another frequently cited argument in favor
of their Portuguese authenticity: as one author put it, the fiery emotions expressed in the letters are so evocative "of this Alentejo soaked in the sun
and *saudade* that no French creature could have written them" (Monteiro
1941, 57).

In Beja itself, the newly invented local tradition took root slowly at
first, but gradually proceeded to acquire a reassuring firmness and an inescapable pervasiveness. The review of Cordeiro's *Soror Mariana* did not

Delfim Guimarães

A Paixão de Soror Mariana

1926
GUIMARÃES & C.ª — Editores
68, Rua do Mundo, 70
LISBOA

The cover of one of the many books published in Portugal that glossed "the passion of
Soror Mariana."

appear in the weekly *O Bejense* until 29 September 1888, well over a month since the book's publication and several weeks after the publishers had gratefully acknowledged their receipt of a copy sent by the author. What is more, the review was merely a reprint of an article earlier published in Lisbon's *Correio da Manhã*, which had already been reinserted in Cordeiro's *Jornal da Noite*. Several decades later, however, Mariana Alcoforado would become a constant presence in Beja's press, as documented by assiduous coverage of new publications referring to the *Lettres portugaises* in the local *Diário do Alentejo*.[9] Alentejan writers joined the swelling ranks of dedicated *alcoforadistas*, most prominent among them Manuel Ribeiro, whose *Vida e Morte de Madre Mariana Alcoforado* (1940) was dedicated to the city of Beja and made many claims evoking the author's local knowledge and regionally authenticated understanding.

Claims and arguments legitimized by local competence were also the distinguishing feature of the book *Mariana Alcoforado* by António Belard da Fonseca (1966), the last study published in Portugal that made a serious, committed case in favor of Portuguese authenticity of the *Lettres portugaises*. True to the pattern established by Cordeiro's *Soror Mariana* and followed by several other subsequent interventions, Fonseca's book was an impassioned response to the publication of a self-described definitive French edition of the letters by Frédéric Deloffre and Jacques Rougeot, whose introductory essay argued conclusively in favor of Guilleragues's authorship. A prominent citizen of Beja, who for many years directed its Museu Regional (located in what remains of Mariana's Convento da Conceição) and who at one time occupied the office of the town's mayor, Fonseca forcefully staked out his claim to local authority in the case, stressing, in addition to his other qualifications, that he lived on the same street where the Alcoforado residence had once been located and was therefore in the physical proximity of the Portuguese Nun's actual birthplace (xvi). Describing his crusade on behalf of Mariana's authorship of the *Lettres portugaises* in the largely indifferent climate of contemporary Portugal as "the last effort of a medieval knight fighting for his lady" (161), Fonseca made clear that his patriotic imperative was motivated, first and foremost, by his regional pride as an Alentejan and a *bejense*:

> If anyone throughout the world remembers Beja, a small town lost on a remote extremity of Europe—although once, two thousand years ago, it used to be one of the most important outposts of the Roman Empire—it is because it remains associated . . . with the name of Mariana. (160)

Interestingly, present-day coverage of Beja by international tourist guidebooks appears to vindicate Fonseca's conviction. In the 1995 English edition of the Michelin guide, the town merits a modest one star on a scale of one to three (deeming it "interesting," but not "worth a journey" or even "a detour"). At the same time, the tradition of the *Lettres portugaises* is cited as its main distinction: "In the world of literary correspondents Beja has been known for three centuries as the town of the Portuguese Religious" (59). The guidebook from the popular *Let's Go!* series follows suit, even as it manages to get most of its facts wrong in its description of Beja's main attraction.[10] In Beja's own local *Turismo* office, an obsequious young man points out destinations of interest, beginning with the museum housed in the Convento da Conceição, "where Soror Mariana wrote her famous love letters," and throughout the town, the Portuguese Nun's presence is as pervasive as it is tastefully discreet. Next door to the convent, the restaurant "Alcoforado" displays a conventionally eclectic decor, the only allusion to its name being an undistinguished mural painting of a yellowed sheet of parchment with a few sentences quoted from one of Mariana's letters. An elegant teahouse on one of the streets of Beja's historic downtown is decorated with reproductions of famous drawings of the nun, extracted from eighteenth- and nineteenth-century editions of the *Lettres portugaises*, and lists, among its sweet specialties, a variety of a popular Portuguese dessert nicknamed "Toucinho do Céu da Soror Mariana." Curiously enough, it is at the museum itself that the legend is given the least emphasis: a modest leaflet available at the entrance resolutely underplays the significance of the memory of Mariana Alcoforado among its many attractions, even as it stands by the authenticity of the tradition.[11]

The ambivalence displayed by the authors of the museum's leaflet points to the often conflicted way in which, in contemporary Portugal, the somewhat disreputable legend of Soror Mariana (disreputable on grounds quite different from the traditional basis in moral rectitude) becomes nevertheless reappropriated because of its continuing appeal in the cultural consumers' market. Thus, in 1994, the *Beja Information Bulletin* would announce a forthcoming publication of a coffee-table book by Alfredo Saramago dedicated to the town's convent, noting that two possible titles were being contemplated: *O Convento da Conceição* or *O Convento de Soror Mariana Alcoforado*. Unsurprisingly, it was on the second title that the publishers decided to settle and the author, sounding almost apologetic in his introduction, supplemented his exhaustive historic and architectural presentation of Beja's chief monument with a final chapter summarizing the story of the Portuguese Nun.[12]

In addition to situating Mariana as a representative *alentejana* and a noteworthy *bejense*, Portuguese *alcoforadista* writers found it necessary to concern themselves as well with a retrieval of all and any available data pertaining to the history of her family. As it happened, the heyday of *alcoforadista* fervor in the first decades of the twentieth century coincided with the vogue enjoyed in Portugal, during the same period, by studies of genealogy, with the publication of *Bibliografia nobiliárquica portuguesa* dating from 1916 (Ramos 1994, 581). Vindicating Eric Hobsbawm's assertion that invented traditions, no matter how recent, require a legitimizing rooting in an immemorial past (1983), one author described the nun as an offspring of the "robust family tree of the Alcoforados, whose ancient roots drew their earliest sustenance from warring tribes established in that part of Iberia which would one day become the Portugal of Afonso Henriques" (Aguiar 1922, 7). In fact, Asdrúbal de Aguiar, whose goal was to support his diagnosis of the Portuguese Nun as a pathological case of "psychological masochism" (6), went on to argue that Mariana simply had to be a masochist in order to justify references to the modesty and inferiority of her condition found in the *Lettres portugaises*. After all, she had no reason to feel overwhelmed by the aristocratic splendor of her French lover, since her family was equal to his in its noble status and superior in ancient origin:

> If a soaring eagle appeared on the Chamilly coat of arms, the emblem of the Alcoforados boasted, against a field of checked blue and white, the same arrogant bird. If Noel was a count, Mariana retained, after taking her vows, the honorific "Dona," which only nuns of noble descent were allowed to use. While Noel gloried in a patrician lineage extending over two hundred years, Mariana could take pride in an ancestry that easily outranked his, as it went back more than six centuries. (70–71)

The issue of social standing of the Alcoforados was, however, far from unequivocally settled. Camilo Castelo Branco, who in the 1870s became the first researcher to inquire into Mariana's genealogy, claimed that her father, Francisco da Costa Alcoforado, had not found it below his station to marry a daughter of a shopkeeper. Arguing vehemently against this assertion, one of the most prominent later *alcoforadistas* contrastively described the nun's maternal grandfather as a "wealthy merchant trading on a large scale" whose designation as a shopkeeper (*tendeiro*) was an injurious slander perpetuated by the anti-*alcoforadista* faction (for whom Camilo had been an acknowledged pioneer) (Ribeiro 1940, 54–56).

Of particular interest to amateur genealogists of the Portuguese Nun proved the possibility of inscribing her unfortunate love story into an explanatory narrative whose diachronic plot could be made to revolve around, as one writer put it, "morbidly amorous tendencies of [her] breed" (Guimarães 1913). While some minor melodramatic episodes in the long history of the family prior to Mariana's own time had been unearthed by avid researchers, the ultimate proof of the Alcoforados' alleged penchant for deviation and morbidity was to be provided by the story of the clan's last offspring, an Alexandre Lobo Alcoforado who had died heirless on 1 February 1879, at the age of forty-two, thus extinguishing his ancient lineage. As the *alcoforadista* tradition has it, Alexandre's father (an only son) was unable to sire any children of his own, which prompted his father who, as the patriarch of the family, felt responsible for preventing its extinction, to have sex with his daughter-in-law in the hope of producing an heir. As a result of this extreme manifestation of what Aguiar called the "degenerative deficiencies" and "abnormalities" ingrained in the family psyche, "the ancient and decaying [family] tree produced one more offspring, but due to the extraordinary conditions of his conception he remained a strange and extravagant creature, psychologically quite abnormal" who ended up dying prematurely "in a hospital cot" (Aguiar 1922, 117–18). Among the many eccentricities apparently evinced by the last *morgado*, one in particular attracted the attention of commentators interested in establishing a retrospective link between his life story and the predicament of Mariana Alcoforado. While studying in Paris during the German siege of 1870, he refused to be drafted into the French army and as a result was expelled from the country by official authorities. As one perspicacious writer went on to suggest, Alexandre's refusal to take up arms in France's defense could in fact be seen as motivated by "a residue of the old animosity felt by the family toward Chamilly's fatherland."[13]

While the Alentejan clan of the Alcoforados may have died out, the mythic narrative of the Portuguese Nun, its by far most famous offspring, was soon to have acquired a compensatory vitality that carried it through the end of the nineteenth and the first decades of the twentieth century on the wings of steadily increasing notoriety. By contrast, in contemporary Portugal, the myth has lost most of it early power (on which more is said in subsequent chapters). Nevertheless, it remains alive and well in a somewhat less exalted form of a depoliticized legend, an appealing tradition no longer concerned with its powerful allegorical potential for explaining the nation's identity and its complicated historical predicament. Thus, to give but one representative example, on 28 July 1995, the Portuguese television channel RTP2 could air an inaugural installment of a travel show called *Viagens na minha terra* and described as "a journey through the country . . . inspired by Almeida Garrett's novel . . . presenting our greatest tourist attractions." The episode, dedicated to the Lower Alentejo, was titled "Mariana's Letters" and, while it went on to document in detail the many architectural and archaeological attractions of Beja and its province, it opened with a distinctly nonrevisionist sequence devoted to the famous nun, complete with camera shots of her celebrated window and loosely qualified by a disclaimer *segundo reza a lenda,* as legend has it. What this manner of presentation demonstrates, beyond confirming the continuing appeal of Mariana's story in the consumers' market of contemporary Portuguese culture, is that the lengthy process of its invention may be considered as substantially completed: the national myth of the Portuguese Nun, a product of many decades of imaginatively creative writing superimposed on scarce and often contradictory historical record, has acquired a reassuring firmness and cohesion of a timeless legend.

3

Translating Mariana

A PARTICULARLY CRUCIAL STAGE IN THE PROCESS OF NATIONAL reappropriation of the *Lettres portugaises*, translation has also necessarily figured as perhaps its most vexed and complicated aspect. After all, it is in the realm of language, translation, and translatability that Mariana's letters appear at their uniquely miscast as an icon of Portugueseness, given the translated text's double linguistic remove from whatever pure distillation of national essence the Portuguese *alcoforadistas* were able to postulate at the source of its primitive expression. In the absence of the vernacular original of the nun's letters, Portuguese translators of the *Lettres portugaises* were faced with a complex task of attempting to recover that lost treasure, although just what exactly would have been its most precious aspect (and therefore what was most worthy of recovery through translation) remained open to debate. In 1888, Luciano Cordeiro, the henceforward undisputed paragon of the *alcoforadista* tradition, made the following comments on the strategy he had pursued in his own translation of the *Lettres*:

> Given the irremediable absence . . . of the original text, it seems of utmost importance to capture and determine the idea, the feeling, the sensory drama, in a word the *soul* that is reflected in these letters through their French version . . . —not the *form*, the language, that which disappeared, vanished, and may only be reconstituted by way of pretentious and useless artifice. (1888, 198; original emphasis)

Cordeiro's criticism, implicit in the conclusion of the above passage, was directed in particular against the earliest Portuguese version of the *Lettres portugaises*, whose author, the neoclassical purist Filinto Elísio, had imbued his translation with an erudite and archaic flavor. Cordeiro, by contrast, subscribed to a dynamic concept of language and to a view of literary communication as irreversibly affected by historical change, arguing in fact that even his own translation should not be considered definitive or exemplary, but merely a step in an ongoing process of reinscribing Mariana's amorous lament into the artistic and spiritual canon of Portuguese national identity. Nevertheless, the possibility and, indeed, inevitability of multiple translations (or "reversions" and "retroversions" as many translators chose to call them) did not make individual efforts seem any less important.[1] At least since Teófilo Braga had discovered in the letters of Mariana Alcoforado a concentrated essence of Portugueseness, the soul of the text became homonymous with the soul of the nation and, as a consequence, translation came to be perceived as an enterprise not only necessary but also deadly serious. In addition to proclaiming the letters to be authentic, Teófilo insisted on their relevance as a quasi-documentary record of the national spirit, unadulterated in that respect by the French mask they were forced to carry: "the Portuguese soul impressed upon the sentiment [of the letters] a form all of its own, which the French words could not obliterate" (1870, 211). At the same time, however, while it became imperative to rescue what was genuinely Portuguese in the letters from underneath their disfiguring French disguise, the existence of multiple translations could not fail to hint at the danger of further adulteration of their hypothetical original purity. As David Lloyd comments, referring to "adulteration as the constitutive anxiety of nationalism," "[f]or the nationalist citizen, the identity of the race is adulterated by 'la belle infidèle' and, as in the old expression, the restoration of that identity by translation (*traduttore*) is haunted by the anxiety of betrayal (*traditore*)" (1993, 106). Of course, Portuguese translators of the *Lettres portugaises* were faced with a particularly convoluted dilemma, for it was precisely the nationally representative (but not nationally targeted and confined) passion of the adulterous Mariana (the original *belle infidèle*) that resulted in the production of the adulterated (French) text. In other words, if the Portuguese Nun's illicit affair with a foreigner had not taken place, there would have been no such thing as the *Lettres portugaises* to begin with, and therefore the text's apparently selfsame national identification had been, from the start, irremediably predicated on the foreign contamination of its source. Denying the letters' constitutive Frenchness might therefore appear tantamount to denying them *tout court*.

It is not my intention in this chapter to carry out a stylistic analysis of subsequent Portuguese "versions" of the French text of the letters, however interesting such an account might prove from the point of view of both historical linguistics and formal theory of translation. "Translating Mariana" will examine instead theoretical and ideological implications stemming from the process of national reappropriation, through translation and commentary, of a text that, although foreign, became naturalized to the point of being declared to represent the purest distillate of the essential characteristics that make Portuguese national identity unique (and therefore also, ironically, untranslatable).

Among Portuguese scholars and critics who over the decades concerned themselves with the linguistic aspect of the nun's letters, a substantial minority attempted to overcome the vexed question of translation as reversion to a hypothetical Portuguese manuscript by declaring that the original language of Mariana's correspondence with Chamilly had to be none other than French. This line of interpretation was pioneered in 1915 by the Count of Sabugosa. The conviction that French was the original language of the *Lettres portugaises* had of course already been voiced in Portugal, most prominently by Camilo Castelo Branco as well as, reportedly, by Alexandre Herculano. Before Sabugosa, however, that claim was always posited as a leading and conclusive argument in the case against the possibility of Mariana's authorship of the letters and in favor of their being a literary fake produced by a French writer. Sabugosa claimed that Mariana, as a daughter of a noble family and a nun in a prominent if provincial convent, was certain to be well educated and that French would have been a natural component of her instruction. More interestingly, he proposed that her putative aptitude towards foreign languages was merely another aspect of her representativeness as Portuguese: "Every Portuguese has a natural talent for foreign languages, and it is well known that for over two centuries our writers were bilingual, employing Portuguese and Spanish in their works with equal success" (261).

On the other hand, as Sabugosa went on to argue, it was also well known that Chamilly had been a man of small intelligence, and as such was unlikely to have learned Portuguese during his sojourn in Beja.[2] In addition, he would not have felt the need to do so since French was widely and readily spoken in Portugal: "Even today, any moderately educated person who wishes to address a Frenchman residing in Portugal will address him in his own language" (262). Finally, Sabugosa pointed out that Sousa Botelho, the first Portuguese proponent of national reappropriation of the *Lettres portugaises*, himself composed introductory remarks to his edition "in the purest French" (262), thus demonstrating "to what extent it is natural for a Portuguese to compose in the French language any statement that is destined to be read by Frenchmen" (265).

Sabugosa's arguments with regard to linguistic prowess and xenophilic adaptability of the Portuguese interestingly echo the German literary historian Friedrich Bouterwek who, writing in his early nineteenth-century *History of Spanish and Portuguese Literature*, analyzed at some length contrasting spiritual and intellectual characteristics of the two peninsular nations. For Bouterwek, one of the reasons for the fact that in the sixteenth and seventeenth centuries many Portuguese poets wrote in Castilian, whereas "nothing could be more extraordinary than to find either verse or prose written in the Portuguese language by a Spaniard" (1823, 52), was the innate "flexibility of the Portuguese character [which] more readily accommodated itself to foreign forms" (54). In other contexts, such protean adaptability to "foreign forms" and the concomitant state of perpetual translation between the self and the world has been amply analyzed, particularly by feminist and postcolonial critics, as resulting from a predicament of political and cultural marginality that makes social and personal advancement contingent on the level of fluency in the dominant idiom a marginalized individual is capable of attaining. This syncretic state of linguistic and cultural hybridization of the "minor" self is, as Abdul R. Jan-Mohamed and David Lloyd point out, "always asymmetrical: although members of the dominant culture rarely feel obliged to comprehend various ethnic cultures, minorities are always obliged, in order to survive, to master the hegemonic culture" (1990, 7).

What holds true for ethnic minorities and colonial and postcolonial societies of the Third World may also, to a variable degree, be demonstrated as valid with regard to such semiperipheral sociopolitical and cultural formations as, among other minor European nations, modern Portugal. It is worth remarking in this context that political and disciplinary collisions between Eurocentric premises of traditional comparative approaches to literary and cultural study and the inherently and necessarily anti-Eurocentric stance of postcolonial politics and theory appear to have colluded towards a subtle yet unmistakable reinforcement of a monolithic and monologic "European" identity, in which the ideal notion of "Europe as Subject" (Spivak 1988, 271), devoid of historical and geopolitical determinants of its own, is mirrored by the oppositional construct of Europe as Object, a staunchly self-identical metropolitan Other to the richly fragmented (post)colonial Self. According to JanMohamed and Lloyd, "when Europeans come together to discuss their various national literatures, they are seen as being able to communicate coherently across linguistic barriers" (1990, 3). Similarly, Richard Jacquemond argues with regard to modern translation theory that, having developed "on the almost exclusive basis of European linguistic and cultural experience, it relies on the implicit postulate of an egalitarian relationship between different linguistic and cultural areas" (1993, 140). Such remarks, myopic for legitimate reasons of their own, nevertheless belie the fact that only a very small, historically variable but relatively stable, minority of European languages and cultures have experienced linguistic and cultural exchange within Europe on an egalitarian basis. When Mariana Alcoforado's last Portuguese champion, António Belard da Fonseca, complained bitterly that the 1962 edition of the *Lettres portugaises* by Deloffre and Rougeot, with its forceful and largely conclusive arguments in favor of French authorship, was likely to be generally accepted, since it was published "in a universally recognized language and by the *Garnier Frères* of Paris" (1966, xvii), he articulated a deep-seated conviction with regard to the predicament of cultural marginality shared by Portugal and the Portuguese language, along with a self-defeating realization that his polemic with the French editors was unlikely to be perceived as a dialogue between equals.[3]

On the other hand, as I have already remarked, Portugal's semiperipheral specificity in the modern age has been rooted in the country's "anomalous" status as, on the one hand, a poor relative among European nations and, on the other, the metropolis of a colonial empire spanning several continents. It is striking to realize, in this context, that the notions of purported innate "flexibility" of Portuguese national character and its high degree of adaptability to "foreign forms" were also employed in the service of the ideology supporting Portuguese colonial expansion overseas, most notably as leading tenets in the influential theory developed by the eminent Brazilian anthropologist and sociologist Gilberto Freyre under the label of *Luso-Tropicalismo*. Freyre coined the term "Luso-Tropicalism" in the years 1930–60 to describe the specificity of Portuguese presence in the tropics; his central claim—that the Portuguese, more than any other European colonizing nation, successfully adapted their civilization to the native reality of the lands they colonized—was eagerly co-opted by Salazar's regime in the 1960s and employed to lend credence to its determination to continue colonial rule in Africa, even as a massive process of decolonization was taking place all over the continent (Wheeler 1993, 117). Freyre's arguments, buttressed by his international scholarly prestige garnered by such influential works as *Casa Grande e Senzala* (1933) and *Sobrados e Mucambos* (1935), could not fail to appear as a godsend to the increasingly embattled ideologues of Portuguese colonialism. As he wrote,

> Unlike the activities of other Europeans in the Tropics, those of the Portuguese have nearly always been an endeavor of great depth and purpose.... [This] mission did not mean subjugating oriental peoples, cultures and values

so that European men, values and imperialist cultures could rule over them, if only superficially; but meant a much more complex process of adaptation, contemporisation, acclimatization and adjustment, in fact, of interpretation of values or cultures, as well as the miscegenation they nearly always practiced. (1961, 32)[4]

It was in another, earlier book, *Aventura e rotina* (subtitled "Suggestions from a trip in search of the constants of Portuguese character and action"), that Freyre briefly crossed paths with the myth of the Portuguese Nun and managed, however implicitly, to integrate the figure of Mariana Alco-forado into the Luso-Tropical scenario he was busy painting. As depicted in *Aventura e rotina*, Alentejo and Beja in particular are a quintessential border zone of transition and translation between Europe and the tropics; it is under the sun of Alentejo that "Portugal first gains a more intense coloring and begins to display its most distinctive traits of a Luso-Tropical, and not merely European, system of landscape, life and culture" (1953, 105). Freyre's observations with regard to the regional characteristics of the province interestingly color his contiguous remarks on the *Lettres portugaises* and their presumed author. While inclining to consider the origin of the text as fictional, he argued that, once published in Portuguese, the letters became organically grafted into the cultural and literary tradition of Portugal, not unlike several of Elizabeth Barrett Browning's *Sonnets from the Portuguese*, which, masterfully translated by the Brazilian poet Manuel Bandeira, "in a way, seem to have *returned* to what is par excellence the language of sonnets and love letters, and not in the least to have *invaded* it as an exotic novelty or an insolent intrusion, in the manner of almost all translation" (104; my emphasis). In other words, Freyre's remarks, read within the larger context of his theory of Luso-Tropicalism, place translatability, understood as both an ability to translate and a susceptibility to being translated, as a central constituent of Portuguese "character and action." Just as translations from, respectively, French and English, of the *Lettres portugaises* and *Sonnets from the Portuguese* were perceived as nonviolent acts of peaceful assimilation due to innate characteristics of the Portuguese language, so too Portuguese expansion overseas appeared to Freyre as an enterprise of caring and careful "interpretation" of the colonial other, made possible by the essential openness and flexibility of the colonizers' national character.

Unlike Freyre, however, most Portuguese *alcoforadistas* and translators of the *Lettres portugaises* saw such nationally characteristic adaptability as a threat more than a virtue, and naturally so, since they viewed it from a perspective of a minor European language and culture locked in a confrontation with the very cultural core of the continent, which, for Portugal, remained firmly located in France at least till the mid-twentieth century, and whose influence was felt at many levels of Portuguese social and cultural reality. Filinto Elísio, who translated the *Lettres portugaises* along with many works of French literature during his Parisian exile, saw it as his mission to de-Gallicize contemporary Portuguese and return it to its exalted roots in the classical cadences of *Os Lusíadas*. As a result, he produced, among other works, a translation of Chateaubriand's *Les Martyrs* (1816) that transposed the French author's Romantic poetic prose into verse in the manner of Camões, employing "the most elevated and resonant words of our language" in order to counter the "barbarous Gallicisms that have distorted it," as he put it in his preface (Buescu 1997, 555).

Filinto's "de-Gallicizing" mission statement may be read alongside one of the important texts of linguistic nationalism on the European periphery, "The Necessity for De-Anglicizing Ireland" (1892) by Douglas Hyde, founder-president of the Gaelic League and a principal advocate of the Irish-language revival (Lloyd 1993, 101). In his essay, Hyde struck an already familiar note in bemoaning "the extraordinary fact that the nation which was once, as every one admits, one of the most classically learned and cultured nations in Europe, is now one of the least so" (153). Not unlike Manuel Bernardes Branco in his *Portugal e os estrangeiros*, he also looked to more geoculturally privileged denizens of the European core for a validation of his claim of ancient Irish glory:

> But the Irish language *is* worth knowing, or why would the greatest philologists of Germany, France, and Italy be emulously studying it, and it *does* possess a literature, or why would a German savant have made the calculations that the books written in Irish between the eleventh and seventeenth century, and still extant, would fill a thousand octavo volumes." (160; original emphasis)

Hyde went on to link this condition to Anglo-Gaelic hybridization of contemporary Irish language and culture, whose permeability, as he prophesied, would ultimately lead the nation into even further decline: "We will become, what, I fear, we are largely at present, a nation of imitators, the Japanese of Western Europe, lost to the power of native initiative and alive only to secondhand assimilation" (169). For Filinto Elísio, as for Hyde nearly a century later, language, translation, and national identity had also been intimately interconnected, and in this he appears, for all his neoclassical fuddy-duddiness, strikingly modern. In fact, it is possible to see in his archaizing translation of the *Lettres portugaises* less an effort to render their presumably original seventeenth century "form" than a striving toward linguistic realization of the national "soul," which for Filinto had attained its highest and therefore most representative expression in the classical idiom of Camões and his followers.[5] In other words, Luciano Cordeiro's criticism, quoted at the beginning of this chapter, may have missed the point to some extent, since Filinto appeared as concerned with adequate representation of the national spirit as later translators of the *Lettres portugaises*; however, by the late nineteenth century it was no longer possible to dress that spirit in unmodified sixteenth- or seventeenth-century garb and even Camões himself had to be reinvented for modern times, as Almeida Garrett had demonstrated in his pioneering Romantic poem *Camões* (1825).[6]

By the first decades of the twentieth century, the growing multiplicity of Portuguese translations of the *Lettres portugaises* could not fail to intensify the anxiety of betrayal and adulteration of the unavailable original text. One way to avoid the anxiety, or at least to relieve its symptoms, was to follow the line of interpretation offered by Sabugosa, and accept French as the original language of the correspondence. Another possibility, proposed by Manuel Ribeiro, was contingent on the adoption of a modified Platonic line of reasoning with regard to the text: the Alentejan writer insisted that even the presumably lost Portuguese original of the letters (in whose existence he believed) was already a translation of sorts. As he put it, "The *Cartas* are . . . symptomatic interpreters of Portuguese uniqueness. In a certain manner, they mirror our qualities, they project us and represent us" (1940, viii). Ribeiro's eminently Platonic vocabulary—interpreting, mirroring, projection, representation—makes it clear that the task of the translator was not to recreate the Portuguese original of the letters, but rather to join that original, along with any number of its translations, in a sort of tangential gathering of more or less accurate mirrors around the invisible center occupied by the national soul.

However, Ribeiro's Platonic stance did more to complicate than to solve the ever-present dilemma. For whether we were to consider Portuguese translations of the *Lettres portugaises* as simulacra (Plato's "bad" images) or as copies ("good" or adequate images)—and Ribeiro clearly saw at least his own effort as a worthy copy of the lost original and of the national essence it had carried within—such reasoning had no choice but to remain rooted in a privileging of "self-identity, similitude, and the order of the same in an absolute sense" (Johnston 1993, 48). This is because, as John

Johnston clarifies, "the resemblance of the copy to the model presumes and is guaranteed by the ontological priority of the self-identical Idea, which necessitates that difference can only appear in a negative and secondary light" (48). Nevertheless, as I have already pointed out, difference, in its concomitant guises of adultery and adulteration, had not merely threatened to invade the story of origin of Mariana's letters, it had in fact always been at the heart of that story's cornerstone argument, a treacherously crumbling center that would never properly hold together the edifice built around it by generations of *alcoforadistas*. Which may help explain why some of the most prominent ideologues of Portuguese cultural nationalism in the early twentieth century, who nevertheless were not willing to abandon the notion of the letters' authenticity and of their rightful place in the national canon, preferred to follow the path laid out by Sabugosa. While accepting French as the original language of the *Lettres portugaises* did nothing to neutralize the narrative's most prominent pitfalls (and indeed added some new hurdles to be overcome by factual arguments in favor of its authenticity), it at least eliminated the awkwardness of viewing Portuguese versions of the letters as twice removed from the original source. Sabugosa himself had presented Mariana as not so much the author as the, so to speak, original translator of her own work, since her heart was certain to have felt, and therefore also spoken, in Portuguese: "She translated herself as she wrote, confused and agitated, while downstairs, at the convent's gate, the Count's messenger impatiently awaited her reply. . . ." (1923, 263).

With Mariana herself, as it were, in charge of the translation, the legitimacy of the French version could be assured, while at the same time the nun's soul was certified as Portuguese-speaking and therefore less liable to the always threatening accusations of unpatriotic dissidence.

Among the translations and comments on translation of the *Lettres portugaises* that belong to the agenda of Portuguese cultural nationalism in the twentieth century, two cases in particular stand out: the remarks of João de Castro Osório, which emphasize the role of translation in the cementing of the Portuguese literary canon, and a 1941 bilingual edition of the letters, produced by Afonso Lopes Vieira in collaboration with the French writer Charles Oulmont. Both Osório and Vieira were prominent participants in the large-scale cultural and artistic movement loosely defined as a *reaportuguesamento* ("relusification") of Portugal, making Portugal Portuguese again. As Rui Ramos describes it, this powerful cultural wave surpassed by far the dimensions of a "simple literary vogue" (570):

It was an industry that had profoundly affected middle-class life. It consisted in bringing back to stage the plays of Gil Vicente, in writing regionalist novels, extolling the Manueline style, building "Portuguese-style houses" (*casas portuguesas*) with porches and ceramic tiles (*azulejos*), furnishing drawing rooms in D. João V style and covering walls with tapestries from Arraiolos and José Malhoa's paintings with scenes from life of the common people.

It is important to caution, following Ramos, against viewing the quest protagonized by the *reaportuguesadores* as provincial or naive. Anchored in the turn-of-the-century reaction against positivist and universalist ideals of the Geração de 70, the movement was very much in tune with internationally prevailing trends of the era. As Eric Hobsbawm describes it, "in the period from 1888 to 1914 nationalism took a dramatic leap forward, and its ideological and political content was transformed" (1987, 142). One of the most significant among those transformations was the invention and/or consolidation of a distinct cultural content that would henceforward lend substance to both high- and low-cultural affirmations of national allegiance; what Ramos succinctly diagnoses as "the emergence of an entity called 'Portugal' in the lives of the Portuguese, from daily routine to politics and artistic creativity" (567). Corresponding closely to similar cultural movements occurring at the same time elsewhere in Europe, it was thus, paradoxically, a cosmopolitan and radically modern intellectual campaign (however strongly allied, for the most part, with a conservative political agenda), whose goals oscillated, sometimes uneasily, between recuperation of the forgotten past and an explicit search for a contemporary artistic synthesis. As such, it was guided by the principle of what David Lloyd calls a " 'translational' aesthetic" of cultural nationalism, according to which "what must be constantly carried over is the essential spirit rather than the superficial forms" of the national culture (1993, 97). Its underlying premise was the conviction that, prior to the emergence of the bourgeois society, there had existed a "Portuguese reality," a way of life that molded itself perfectly to the national character and that was lost when members of the Portuguese middle class began to imitate slavishly their European homologues. Since the physical realia that had constituted and supported the uniquely and ideally Portuguese way of life no longer existed, save for isolated traces to be found in historical legends, ingrained habits of country life, or certain pervasive constants of national psychology, such as *saudade*, it was necessary, as the *reaportuguesadores* argued, to combine an archaeological prowess with an effort of translational imagination in order to recreate the Old Portugal into a new *pátria* for the modern age.

One of the protagonists of the *reaportuguesamento* campaign on the front of Portuguese literature was João de Castro Osório, a critic and historian best remembered nowadays in connection with the original publication of Camilo Pessanha's *Clepsidra* (1920). Among his many scholarly endeavors one finds a curious compilation entitled *Florilégio das poesias portuguesas escritas em castelhano e restituídas à língua nacional* (1942). As the title indicates, Osório devoted his creative energies to the recovery, or "restitution" (the rhetoric of property being entirely adequate here) of poems written in Spanish by writers whom he identified as Portuguese nationals. In his preliminary remarks, Osório made a radical claim with regard to cultural disparity between the two peninsular nation-states, arguing in effect that in the entire Western world there are to be found no two national "spirits" (*génios*) more distinct from one another than the Spanish and the Portuguese (7). He went on to harangue against what he referred to as "the alleged bilingualism of Portuguese literature" prior to the eighteenth century (18): according to Osório, a work of literature was either Portuguese or it was not, regardless of the language in which it was written, and the distinguishing criterion should rely on a determination whether an author adopted the idiom he used in his work as a "national language" or an "artistic language" (19).[7] When using a foreign language as an "artistic" mode of expression, the writer did so at his peril, but could still be successful in negotiating the obstacle course that his choice had created:

> He may become denationalized and, above all, render his work sterile due to its fundamentally artificial nature. But, even so, he will not necessarily lose his national identity, nor will his works cease to belong–in many cases quite justifiably and grandly so–to the literature of the Nation whose son he is. (20)

Osório's enterprise was of course profoundly and resolutely anachronistic, since full coincidence, as opposed to haphazard overlapping, of a writer's provenance, his or her language, and national identification (if any) had been a quite recently invented notion. Not until Johann Gottfried Herder's writings in the second half of the eighteenth century had language been placed squarely at the emotional and intellectual center of modern nationalism's concern for authenticity. As Joshua Fishman comments, Herder's thought proved most influential in "developing the complementary views that the mother tongue expressed a nationality's soul or spirit, [and] that since it was a collective achievement par excellence, language was also the surest way for individuals to safeguard (or recover) the authenticity they had inherited from their ancestors as well as to hand it on to generations yet unborn. . . ." (1973, 46). By contrast, in the Portuguese sixteenth and seventeenth centuries (the period most forcefully targeted by Osório), such ideas had little currency, although some preliminary manifestations of linguistic nationalism could of course be registered, particularly in the context of Portugal's loss of independence to Spain (1580–1640). Even then, however, Portuguese-Castilian diglossia was so widespread and so (relatively) independent of the ideological stance assumed by a given Portuguese writer that many authors chose to chronicle in the language of the enemy the progress of their country's prolonged war against Spain in the mid-seventeenth century. Even more remarkably, a number of Portuguese theater plays celebrating the victory of the liberationist movement, with triumphalist titles such as *La mayor hazaña de Portugal* by Manuel Araújo de Castro (1645) or *Restauración de Portugal* by Manuel de Almeida Pinto (1649), were both written and performed in Spanish. Not to mention that the *Restaurador* himself, the Duke of Bragança, would write, nine years after his acclamation as João IV, the new king of independent Portugal, a *Defensa de la Música Moderna* in purest Castilian (Cuesta 1988, 141–42).

As for the *Lettres portugaises*, what Osório had to say about the work in his lengthy introduction to the *Florilégio* was that this quintessential case of nationally pertinent content obscured by the cloak of foreign linguistic expression was also a rare one, since "[a] work written in a language foreign to the author's national character is normally a failed one" (1942, 27). He extended his heavily qualified diagnosis of Soror Mariana's letters as artistically successful to a few other works such as, most notably, the pastoral novel *Diana* (1559) by Jorge de Montemor, better known by the Castilian version of his name as Jorge de Montemayor. What, for Osório, elevated aesthetic quality of those texts to a superior level was the degree in which they had managed to retain demonstrable traces of their true national affiliation: "The truly beautiful works written by Portuguese authors in ancient or foreign languages are beautiful precisely insofar as they reveal our national character" (27). Therefore, as Osório went on to argue in support of his translational (or "restitutional") endeavor, even the least polished Portuguese versions of such texts were certain to be more appealing than their "foreign" originals, since translation activated what the author called their "virtual beauty": "Reverted into the Portuguese in which they had been thought out, they appear to us in greater depth and beauty. Naturally; of themselves; by their own national quality rather than by the grace of their translator's labor" (29).

Osório's comments exhibit throughout a sternly moral stance: a writer's use of a language other than his national idiom is "in principle . . . the greatest sin that he can commit against his Nation and the greatest error with regard to his own work" (18). However, in considering the exceptional nature of the *Lettres portugaises*, he was forced to stand his leading argument on its head, since it had been precisely an act of "antinational" linguistic adulteration (as well as adultery, an aspect which Osório chose not to tackle) that gave Mariana's love lament its international fame and thus turned it into a "pronational" agent of cultural expansion and influence. According to the critic, the letters of the Portuguese Nun

> let a new spirit be heard in France, spirit none other than that of all our love poetry. And it was this novelty, this new and strange voice, that fomented (as would have done, and better, much of our literature, had it been translated into French) a sentimental revolution, so much so that they were pointed to as having influenced Jean Racine, the French poet of feminine love. (27–28)

In other words, if the *Lettres portugaises* had been written and disseminated exclusively in Portuguese, their patriotic value, if any, would have been greatly reduced. Osório, however, managed to skip over the dangerous implications carried by his comments and went on to thunder against his chosen kind of ideological culprit: the "mistaken . . . and dangerous . . . notion that our literature is not intimately and exclusively linked to one language only—the Portuguese" (30). Interestingly, the peril implicit in such a misguided idea was related by the author to the historical and contemporary identity of Portugal as the metropolis of a transnational empire; since it was the Portuguese language that guaranteed the cultural unity of the Lusophone world, colonial and postcolonial alike, it must be protected from any assaults that would threaten to disturb its centrality, in Portugal itself, as the main guarantor of national authenticity.

A *reaportuguesador* considerably more eminent than João de Castro Osório, Afonso Lopes Vieira was described by a latter-day encomiast as someone who "[perhaps] more than anyone else . . . pursued untiringly . . . a sum total of Portugal and Portugueseness" (Quadros 1989, 136), while some of Vieira's contemporaries had exalted in him "the guardian of Portuguese lyricism" and "the Grand Master of Portugueseness" (Pereira 1979, 75–76).[8] Similarly to Osório, Vieira was also adamant about the need for "restitution" of national texts written in foreign languages. Two of his most prominent efforts in that direction were the translations into Portuguese of the medieval *Romance de Amadis* (1922) and of Montemor's *Diana* (1924), both presented by the author as texts that "enveloped Lusian sensibility in Castillian rhythms" (Montemor, iii–iv).[9] At the same time, however, Vieira was considerably less sanguine about the possibility of submitting the *Lettres portugaises* to a similar "relusifying" treatment. In an essay published in 1922, the year of the publication of his greatly popular rendition of *Amadis*, he went as far as to declare that Mariana Alcoforado herself would not have been able to translate her own letters: "In this most singular case of the *Cartas*, we may claim, without fearing appearance of a paradox, that not even the nun herself, had she wished to translate her own letters, would have been able to carry over that which makes them so unique and enchanting" (257). Where others placed prolific translatability and eagerness to translate at the core of Portuguese national character, Vieira pursued a different line of interpretation. Summing up his critique of existing Portuguese translations, or "versions," of the *Lettres portugaises*, he likened them to instruments of torture inflicted upon the vulnerable corpus that in his phrasing appears as the body of the nun inextricably fused with the body of her text: "And this is how the poor and adorable Mariana . . . was submitted through translation to almost as many tortures as those she had suffered from Chamilly" (259). Vieira set out plainly the reasons for such persistent inadequacy of successive translations: the letters were pure lyricism and lyricism, the essence of Portuguese national soul, is by definition untranslatable, *even into Portuguese*. As he noted further, such was also the fundamental reason for lack of international recognition traditionally suffered by Portuguese literary masterpieces: "What the world knows of our lyrical Soul has been nearly always but pale reflected moonlight" (256).

The fear of paradox evoked by Vieira was of course a luxury that the *reaportuguesador* in him could not afford, engaged as he was in attempting to translate for the modern age precisely that which he and others repeatedly identified as untranslatable, the essential qualities of the Lusitanian "race." And so, two decades after he had pronounced Mariana's letters as resistant to translation in the highest degree, Vieira went on to translate them himself. The interest of his 1942 edition, however, does not lie primarily in its presenting a yet another Portuguese version of the French text, but rather in its unique conceptual and editorial design. Vieira subscribed to the Sabugosa thesis in considering French as the original language of the correspondence, but the scenario he envisioned nevertheless involved translation, albeit of the intralingual variety, in Roman Jakobson's terminology (1987):

> The letters must have been written in French. . . . But in the capital of the *precieuses* Mariana's French was not presentable. In the Alentejan wilderness of her convent, the poor girl ignored subtle rules of language that reigned in Rambouillet. It therefore became necessary to polish her enchanting roughness and to correct the natural disorder. The publisher Barbin put the writer Guilleragues in charge of editing the text, barbarous and bursting with life. (10–11)

Vieira's own Portuguese translation of the *Lettres portugaises* (or, as he modestly called it, a "textual attempt") became thus akin to his earlier "versions" from the Spanish of *Amadis* and *Diana*, an adaptation or paraphrasis performed with an eye on adequate rendition of the "national sentiment . . . throbbing underneath the foreign language" (13). His bilingual edition did, however, contain another transformed version of the published French text: Vieira's collaborator, Charles Oulmont, produced what he saw as a first step toward a reconstitution of Mariana Alcoforado's "adorably rough" original expression. Oulmont's chief task was, as he described it, to eliminate "the precious bits," presumably introduced by Guilleragues in order to approximate the discourse of the letters to the French literary taste of the time, as well as to reduce what Oulmont perceived as their "vulgar sensuality" (27–29). The French author's rewriting of the *Lettres portugaises* also aimed, similarly to Vieira's, at highlighting the traces of Portugueseness immanent in the text: in his introduction he cited a number of "portugalismes" he had detected in the French original (36–39). However, the ultimate goal of his intralingual translation was, as he declared, to restore the putative "suppleness" of Mariana's "French Portuguese language" in all its primitive "painful complexity" (40). Oulmont's curious experiment was thus, in the end, distinctly and radically at odds with ideological premises of the cultural campaign of *reaportuguesamento*, insofar as he found the true identity of the *Lettres portugaises* neither in the text's Portugueseness nor in its Frenchness, but rather in the inextricable entanglement of its intercultural miscegenation. What the Vieira-Oulmont edition brings into focus more clearly than perhaps any other "reversion" of the letters is therefore the realization that attempting to erect any monolithic representation of national identity on the foundation of a text as slippery and unreliable as the *Lettres portugaises* was tantamount to asking for a proliferation of disasters. Notwithstanding Oulmont's curious contribution (whose implications he may not have fully realized), it was not until the publication of *Novas Cartas Portuguesas* in 1972 that the translational potential carried by the seventeenth-century text and its convoluted history became fully and compellingly explored.

In conclusion, the unlikely marriage between a slim collection of seventeenth-century love letters written by a lapsed nun to her French *amant* and the cultural agenda of modern Portuguese nationalism created a scene of translation defined by contradiction, ambivalence, and the ever-present anxiety of betrayal. Considering that adulteration (as well as adultery) results in multiplication of possibility, as opposed to linear transmission of verifiable content, such an outcome was indeed inevitable, even though (or perhaps precisely because) the goal of the majority of Portuguese translations of the *Lettres portugaises* was to deny contradiction and erase the stigma of adulteration (not to mention adultery) that the love letters of Mariana Alcoforado have carried into the national literary canon.

4

Canonizing Mariana

I<small>F, AS</small> B<small>ENEDICT</small> A<small>NDERSON AND OTHERS HAVE ARGUED, NATION IS AN</small> imaginary construct predicated on retrospection and invention of tradition, the same has even more clearly been true of national literature, particularly as represented by the national literary canon. Indeed, granting, with Marshall Brown, that literary history is an oxymoron (since linguistic, and particularly literary, expression is in its essence "change, development, innovation" and therefore any theory of expression—including literary history—is possible only as "a theory of the incalculable" [1992, 22]), national literary history stands out as a doubly oxymoronic endeavor, a forced merging of two disparate imaginary dimensions on the basis of a historical record whose reassuring firmness tends to be likewise, more often than not, a figment of the imagination. Yet it is precisely the concept of nationally specific literary canon that has been given, from the early nineteenth century onward, a central place in the articulations of nationness and a crucial function in the forging of a homogeneous collective consciousness, classroom study of great national authors becoming "one of the main instruments employed to shape the young citizen in the official image of the community" (Guillén 1971, 500).

It can hardly be considered a random accident of history that the discovery, translation, and eventually eager adoption of the *Lettres portugaises* by the Portuguese coincided chronologically with the rise of modern cultural nationalism, and specifically with gradual assembling and legitimization of one of its fundamental institutions, national literary history. In the neighboring Spain, as Claudio Guillén describes it, sometime after 1750 a tendency became widespread "to liberate poetry from the domination of unitary, unchanging norms (from an absolute poetics), and to place it under the tutelage of national history. . . . Before this, one could encounter, to be sure, much pride in the Spanish *poets*. It was understood that there were worthy representatives of Spain on Mount Parnassus. But there was, so to speak, only one Parnassus" (501). The partition of Mount Parnassus along national borders became a legacy that, notwithstanding the counter-current of comparative universalism (already well manifest in early Romantic thought), would decisively shape formulations of collective self-knowledge over the following two centuries, as it conceived "the re-sponsibility of literature, and of other cultural forms, to be the production and mediation of a sense of national identity" (Lloyd 1987, xi).

As elsewhere in Europe, so too in Portugal, the emergence of narrative and ideologized histories of national literature was preceded and made possible by the antiquarian labor of anthologists and compilers of biblio-graphic evidence. Diogo Barbosa Machado's monumental *Bibliotheca Lusitana*, published between 1741 and 1759, was the first extensive database providing an indispensable factual repository for future genera-tions of scholars. Unsurprisingly, given its publication date, Machado's en-cyclopedic treasury contained no mention of the *Lettres portugaises*. Neither did any reference to the text appear in the first properly historical overviews of Portuguese literary tradition, both penned by foreigners: the second volume of Friedrich Bouterwek's *History of Spanish and Por-tuguese Literature* published in the original German in 1804 and in the En-glish translation in 1823, and the final five chapters of J. C. L. Simonde de Sismondi's *Historical View of the Literature of the South of Europe* (origi-nally published in 1813 as *De la littérature du midi de l'Europe*; English translation 1827). Scholarly recognition of the letters as properly and le-gitimately Portuguese required that Boissonade's 1810 revelation and sub-sequent translations into their presumably original idiom be taken up by the newly developing narrative of national literary history: as poetic jus-tice would have it, it befell a Frenchman, Ferdinand Denis, with his *Résumé de l'histoire littéraire du Portugal*, published in 1826, to not only produce the first historical investigation devoted exclusively to the study of Portuguese literature (with an appended *resumé* dedicated to Brazilian letters), but also to pioneer the process of reappropriation of the *Lettres portugaises* as a national masterpiece and an eloquently representative showcase of the Lusitanian soul.

As Denis's work clearly demonstrates, the structural move from ency-clopedic to narrative literary history was paralleled by a paradigm shift with respect to the nature of explanatory discourse employed in describing and relating the objects of literary-historical narrative. That discourse became now firmly contextual, that is, based on the premise that, as the author expressed it in his preliminary remarks, "literature walked hand in hand with politics" (vii) and that individual authors and their works were demonstrably and inextricably enmeshed in the social and political fabric of their time.[1] The historical setting of the *Lettres portugaises* was the Portuguese seventeenth century, a period whose overall significance had already been declared as the time of generalized decadence by writers speaking from a common ideological platform in Enlightenment and Romantic liberalism. According to the liberal view, "the two great enemies of man's freedom and, consequently, of the flourishing of culture and the arts, are royal tyranny and Inquisitorial despotism allied with religious obscurantism" (Silva 1971, 164), historical phenomena that were considered decisive determinants of the Portuguese seventeenth century, along with the country's sixty-year loss of independence to Spain.[2]

The first three historians of Portuguese literature show themselves already firmly in agreement with regard to their highly negative diagnosis of *seiscentismo*, denying its literary production not merely aesthetic, but likewise any significant moral or political value, and differing merely in the degree of their contempt for the period's protagonists and their works. Bouterwek's relatively full and evenhanded account is punctuated by a crescendo of ominous subtitles: "Decay of the ancient national energy in Portuguese Literature" (273); "Further decline of Portuguese taste" (302); and finally the apocalyptic "Total Decay of Portuguese Literature towards the end of the Seventeenth Century" (329). Sismondi follows closely upon his predecessor's steps, and so does Denis, with one significant exception: the lovely and moving *Lettres portugaises*, whose existence he is the first to acknowledge and to describe as "the only one [among the poetic works of that period] that truly contains poetry, although it is written in prose" [le seul (parmi les ouvrages poétiques de ce temps) où il y ait vraiment de la poésie, quoiqu'il soit écrit en prose (400)]. Denis, however, gave full credit for the restoration of the *Lettres* to their rightful national context to Sousa Botelho and his 1824 pioneering "retranslation"; and the twin labors of the French Lusophile and the aristocratic Portuguese expatriate thus jointly inaugurated the enterprise of national reappropriation of Mariana's letters. The vicissitudes of that process can oftentimes be shown to support Claudio Guillén's suggestion with regard to potentially compensatory function of newly emerging national literatures, both in the sense, generally recognized, of nationalist ideologies functioning as substitutes for waning religious faiths, and also in a more elusive way: to what extent was the pioneering emergence of the idea of national literature in Italy "a response to the economic and political decline of the Italian states?" (Guillén, 500). Similar decline of the Portuguese state since the seventeenth century was compounded by the growing awareness of the country's peripheral position in Europe, a point brought home by, among other evidence, minimal to nonexistent interest taken in Portugal by the writers of general histories of European letters. Casual commentators reflected this scholarly consensus: elaborating, in 1856, on "Portugal's Glory and Decay," Thomas Wentworth Higginson had this much to say about the country's literature (with the sole exception of Camões):

> To give a survey of Portuguese literature would require the microscopic industry of that unfortunate Bettinelli, whose "fifty-six primary sonneteers" are embalmed in Sydney Smith's satire. Adamson has gone far in that direction, but has produced nothing from all his poets comparable to Elizabeth Barrett's imaginary sonnets from the Portuguese. (474)[3]

Higginson would have done better to refer instead to Longfellow's *The Poets and Poetry of Europe* (1845), with its unusually generous attention bestowed on Portugal, won by the author against objections of his publisher, who had suggested eliminating the Portuguese section altogether (Monteiro 1996, 83–84). It is worth observing, however, that Higginson's privileging of Barrett Browning's "Portuguese" poetic fiction over genuinely Portuguese products illuminates to a considerable extent the troubled history of reappropriation of the internationally renowned *Lettres portugaises* for the national literary treasury: a compensatory gesture against the overwhelming tide of oblivion and contempt sweeping towards Portugal from the European cultural and political center.

By 1845, when Francisco Freire de Carvalho's modest and self-consciously titled *Primeiro Ensaio sobre História Literária de Portugal* was published in Lisbon, the awareness of the letters' existence in their presumed country of origin had become widespread enough for the author to mention Mariana Alcoforado in his section on the epistolary, where he noted, however, that she was "better known among foreigners than among her compatriots" (163), an observation that would become something of a reproachful leitmotiv in nineteenth-century Portuguese references to the prodigious nun.

Denis's enthusiastic paragraphs and Carvalho's single-sentence citation thus initiated over a century and a half of literary historical writing attempting to inscribe the *Lettres portugaises* within the cultural narrative of the nation, or, conversely, aiming to deny them national legitimacy and pertinence. Textual strategies employed by Portuguese writers in their references to the letters, varied as they have been, may be usefully illuminated by employing the notion of "sociogram," coined by Lawrence Buell and described as "the single most fundamental convention in national historiography" and "one of the most stable devices in the literary historiographical repertoire for interlacing text and context" (1993, 222). A sociogram is a formula by which an individual literary work is integrated into a larger literary historical narrative: it consists in "the encapsulated formulation of a work's significance as historical artifact and national product" (222). Sociogrammatic method is the common ground shared by such seemingly divergent readings of Twain's *Connecticut Yankee* (Buell's test case) as those offered, respectively, in the early twentieth-century *Cambridge History of American Literature*, the mid-century *Literary History of the United States* and the contemporary *Columbia Literary History of the United States*. In spite of their differences, all three histories present Twain's work, in a didactic manner, as a sort of social parable; and, while colliding on specifics of its message, they "collude in reading *Yankee* as a symptomatic ideological artifact" and offer an appraisal of the tale "as a microcosm or refraction of its era" (221–22).

In a similar fashion, the respective chapters, subchapters or paragraphs of comprehensive and partial Portuguese literary histories dealing with the *Lettres portugaises* tend to carry verdicts of ideological significance that surpass potentially crippling limitations imposed by the issue of authenticity. The most widely used contemporary one volume handbook, António José Saraiva's and Óscar Lopes's *História da Literatura Portuguesa*, while accepting without reservations the apocryphal identity of the letters, places the mention of their presumed female author as a centerpiece of a paragraph devoted to literary reflexes of the intellectual and social situation of women in seventeenth-century Portugal. Mariana's love letters, however fictional, become a symptomatic epitome of a rebellious, emancipatory attitude that, in historical reality, manifested itself most visibly in the activities of conventual communities of women, leading to repeated conflicts with ecclesiastic authorities and eventually expressing itself in such later "feminist and liberal" literary statements as *Aventuras de Diófanes* by Teresa Margarida da Silva e Orta, first published in 1752 (1987, 499).

Where Saraiva and Lopes bypass the issues of authenticity and foreign provenance by way of ascribing to the *Lettres portugaises* a sort of retroactive ideological significance in their interpretation of materially and nationally specific historic reality, other contemporary Portuguese literary historians find themselves unable to surmount the epistemological obstacle presented by French authorship of the letters. Yet even where present merely by acknowledged omission, references to the *Lettres* still tend to carry a didactic message with distinctly national overtones: most typically, a lesson in antinationalist disillusion and humility. In the recently published literary *Enciclopédia Verbo*, the entry *"Cartas portuguesas"* (by Cristina Almeida Ribeiro) carries at the outset an admonition that the controversy surrounding the text presents "serious doubts as to the pertinence of its inclusion in a history of [Portuguese] literature" (Ribeiro 1995, 1004) and concludes by mildly reproaching national literary tradition for its "stubborn insistence on claiming [the work] as its own" (1007). Andrée Crabbé Rocha is more severely critical in her anthologic overview of the epistolary genre in Portugal. The chief purpose of the brief chapter devoted to the *Lettres portugaises* is for the author to point out the reasons why their analysis does not belong in her study and to conclude by describing them as a false mirror in which "the Portuguese have searched in vain for their own reflection and foreigners have discovered a mythic Portugal" (1965, 196).

The literary historical fortune of the *Lettres portugaises* in Portugal as a work both distinguished and nationally significant—in other words, as charged with "sociogrammatic" prominence—first took full shape in the writings of Teófilo Braga, the nineteenth century's most tireless researcher of Portuguese cultural patrimony. While the preoccupation with recuperating and preserving in national memory of what was uniquely and specifically "Portuguese" may be said to have begun in earnest with Almeida Garrett's *Romanceiros* (1843–1851), their author renounced, however, any pretensions to scholarly criticism and historicist exactitude of record. Distancing himself from "philologists and antiquaries," he relegated to "the academies" the goal of producing "chronological and critical dissertations for the use of scholars" (1966, 679), choosing to act as a humble messenger delivering into the hands of his middle-class readers a simple transcription of "the great national book that is the people and their traditions" (682). It thus befell Teófilo to become the first (not to mention also the most prolific) prominent scholar of what can be properly labeled as national literary history. His trajectory of scholarly writing clearly illustrates a transition from antiquarian labor of compilation (exemplified both by *Bibliotheca Lusitana* and, *mutatis mutandis*, by Garrett's anthologies of popular poetry) to positivist emphasis on scientifically legitimized structuring and interpretation of the historical record. Influenced by Pierre Laffitte, a disciple of Comte, and himself a member of international societies propagating Comtean positivism, Teófilo advocated the establishment in Portugal of a "cult of great men as a means to producing the *pátria*, the social organization judged by Comte as indispensable for the 'normalization' of humanity" (Ramos 1994, 64). His research into popular Portuguese customs, beliefs, and traditions was aimed at establishing "positive bases of nationality" (65) and similar goals guided his interpretation of literary periods, authors, and individual works. In fact, as Eduardo Lourenço argues, Teófilo was almost singlehandedly responsible for the "invention" of Camões as a national writer (1992, 138–50); while the poet's prominent and exemplary stature had been axiomatically accepted in his native land long before the nineteenth century, his figure had tended to be regarded "in a kind of timeless isolation or from an abstract perspective, [as a] stereotypified 'Prince of Lusitanian poets'" (Lourenço, 138), a shortcoming which Teófilo set out to correct in his *História de Camões* (1873), among other works.[4]

It is interesting to observe that what made Camões the lyric poet just as powerfully and uniquely representative of Portugueseness as Camões the epic bard of *Os Lusíadas* resided, for Teófilo, not so much in the poet's intermittent formal allegiance to his native poetic tradition as in his sublime ability to express love Portuguese-style. As Lourenço notes,

> In this national inspiration, Teófilo Braga sees less a particular thematic focus or a consciously adopted legacy of poetic forms and techniques than a *sui generis* deep-rooted affinity with the psychology and the way of being profoundly characteristic of the Portuguese soul. The lyric Camões founds his justification as an heir and greatest poet of the *innate amorous vocation* of the Portuguese people. (144; original emphasis)

Given Teófilo's privileging of romantic love in his characterization of the Portuguese *génio*, or national character (a claim he would reiterate insistently throughout his writings), it is no wonder that he had only words of highest praise for another soon-to-be canonical literary distillation of the national soul. Already in one of his earliest works, *Estudos da Edade Média* (1870), Teófilo dedicated a separate chapter of substantial length to the *Lettres portugaises*, claiming that "in a book that studies works of art according to the spirit of race and nationality, these *Cartas* figure as a profoundly truthful document. Here is the Peninsular soul in its fiery exuberance" (184). Despite the gushing idealism of his central claim, Teófilo's sociogrammatic encapsulation of the letters' national significance took as its point of departure a far more materially precise argument: the chapter opens with the author's denunciation of persistent ill fortune suffered by Portuguese literature, unable to present a claim to lawful possession of some of its most exquisite creations, such as, along with the *Lettres portugaises*, the medieval *Romance de Amadis*. Teófilo blamed "our carelessness" for the loss of the Portuguese manuscript of the letters, insisting that he would never tire of "reclaiming what is ours . . . against the perfidy of foreign bibliographers" (183–84). Mariana's letters became thus an epitome of national identity in a double, complementary (and compensatory) sense: a triumphantly successful reflection of its essence and a bitter, if also rousing, reminder of the country's historical misfortune and cultural marginality exemplified by the ability of mightier nations to rob Portugal of its artistic treasures.

Teófilo retaliated against this vicious circle of Portuguese inferiority on the international scene by producing a circular argument of his own in favor of the letters' authenticity. Since the "adventurous and amorous" nature of the Lusitanian folk had been widely acknowledged throughout Europe (to document this claim, Teófilo lined up all the usual suspects who at one time or another cast a Portuguese as a figure distinguished by a particular susceptibility to lovesickness, from Lope de Vega to Mme de Sévigné and Balzac), it is then incontrovertible that the exquisite amorous discourse of the letters had to originate in Portugal. The eminent historian would have doubtlessly been quite disturbed to learn that a few decades later the exact same premise would be employed by scholars arguing for apocryphal origin of the letters.[5]

If *Estudos da Edade Média* marked Teófilo's first attempt at inscribing the *Lettres portugaises* into the Portuguese literary canon and declaring them a prominent piece of the nation's spiritual heirloom, it was in a later work, *Manual da História da Literatura Portuguesa* (1875), that he made his most notoriously hyperbolic claim regarding their canonical status. Even more significantly, the same claim planted the text firmly in its presumed historical and cultural seventeenth-century context, thus fulfilling a crucial function of sociogrammatic presentation. Teófilo in fact concluded his chapter on the *seiscentistas* with a discussion of the letters, declaring them—in a vein already suggested by Ferdinand Denis half a century earlier—as "the only truly felt, truly beautiful product that the Portuguese soul brings forth in the seventeenth century" (404). By the time a much revised and amplified version of Teófilo's study was published as *Os seiscentistas*, the third volume of his definitive *História da Literatura Portuguesa* (1916), his interpretation of the period had become somewhat more moderate and generous in its appraisal of specific aspects of seventeenth-century literary production. Even so, Mariana's letters retained their prominent and exceptional status as, according to the revised version, "the *most* truly felt psychological document representing the Portuguese soul in the seventeenth century" (1984, 476; my emphasis).

If Teófilo's emphatic, even somewhat extravagant insistence on the letters' representativeness as a national literary artefact secured for them a prominent place in the newly assembled and about to be cemented Portuguese canon, it also contributed, by the sheer peremptoriness of his claims, to inflame the controversy surrounding the legitimacy of their canonic status. The most notable early demonstration of the anti-*alcoforadista* stance (prior to the reopening of scholarly debate that followed the publication of F. C. Green's article in 1926) may be described as a mere skirmish in a large-scale ideological battle for the soul of the nation, which involved Portuguese intellectuals in the first decades of the twentieth century and whose impact has continued to be felt through the years of Salazar's dictatorship and beyond.

A thorough reinterpretation of Portuguese national identity, relying on sources both historical and literary, was one of the chief intellectual goals of the neomonarchic and Catholicist movement Integralismo Lusitano, best illustrated by the writings of its principal doctrinaire António Sardinha. Founded in 1913 by Sardinha, Alberto Monsaraz, and Hipólito Raposo, the group began publishing its periodical, *A Nação Portuguesa*, in 1914 and by the end of the decade could boast a considerable following documented by the proliferation of newspaper articles, publications, and conferences aimed at winning the young generation of Portuguese intellectuals away from the liberal republicanist tradition rooted in political and cultural movements of the nineteenth century. Sardinha and his followers dedicated themselves to a general rewriting of Portuguese history, founding in Integralismo, as Rui Ramos describes it, "a historical school that, guided by a methodological reliance on documentary erudition, set out to correct the liberal version of history" (1994, 543). A radical example of historical revisionism promoted by the Integralists may be found in their reinterpretation of the Portuguese Discoveries. As AbdoolKarim Vakil states, "defining Tradition in terms of a ruralist political ideal modelled on medieval corporative monarchy, Portuguese Integralism emphatically denounced the 'Discoveries' as an 'error,' and as one of the root causes of the capitalist cosmopolitan modernity they so radically opposed" (1996, 49).[6]

Among other polemical interventions, the Integralists became responsible for initiating a modern reevaluation of *seiscentismo*, an intellectual effort whose underpinnings were clearly partisan, as part of a wholesale, antiliberal self-described "counterrevolution," but whose long-term effects may be compared, *mutatis mutandis*, to those of the contemporaneous Spanish celebrations of the tricentenary of Góngora, which contributed decisively toward redeeming the artistic and intellectual legacy of Peninsular

Baroque. Here as elsewhere, Sardinha's insistence on an empirical view of history proved to be a source of richly contradictory effects when confronted, in his writings, with the idealistic opportunism inherent in the brand of cultural nationalism promoted by Integralismo and eloquently defined by another gifted polemicist linked to the movement, Alfredo Pimenta: "In the History of Portugal, everything is true that dignifies the Portuguese Nation; everything is false that debases, diminishes, weakens, or tarnishes her" (quoted in Carvalho 1994, 52). Such contradictions beset also the most militant and lively installment in the 1920s' debate over the significance of the Portuguese seventeenth century, *O Seiscentismo em Portugal* by Manuel Múrias, whose very epigraph (citing Camilo Castelo Branco, the chosen precursor of antiliberal revisionists) proposed to "restore the truth, extricating it from emotional disputes that take root in the field of politics" (1923, 9). Evoking one's abhorrence of "politics" as a preliminary to one's own eminently political argument is of course one of the oldest tricks in the bag. Múrias does not disappoint in this respect, peppering his exposé with frequent references to the contemporary Portuguese political scene: for example, his heated defense of Inquisitorial indices leads him to promote general desirability of central censorship and to propose the establishment of a national Censorship Board (20). On a larger scale, however, his and others' occasionally self-conscious vacillation between professed desire for absolute historical truth and the (also acknowledged) militant subjectivism of the version of truth being promoted prefigures the now common recognition of theorists of literary history concerning the "impossible," aporetic, and oxymoronic nature of the genre, irredeemably suspended between fact and fiction. As David Perkins presents it, "theorists are virtually unanimous in regarding literary histories as, at best, merely hypothetical representations . . . provisional statements in our ongoing dialogue with the past and with each other about the past. . . . And yet, most literary historians also imply, tacitly, that the past has a being, a reality, was so and not otherwise" (1992, 14).[7]

The fact that the Integralists attributed very nearly everything that, according to them, went wrong with the Portuguese nineteenth century to the noxious influence of French political culture on Portuguese *estrangeirados*, who had been eager to emulate the ideas of the Enlightenment and of the French Revolution, was the principal founding irony of the movement (as well a further source of much of its ambivalence), since their own political and intellectual orientation owed its definition and articulation in great measure to the writings of the Frenchman Charles Maurras, the leader of the monarchic, "counterrevolutionary" movement of Action Française founded in 1899. Among Maurras's many works carrying his agenda of monarchism, Catholicism, and extreme economic and cultural nationalism was *Le Romantisme féminin*, a long essay included in his 1905 book *L'avenir de l'intelligence*. As Louis Menand summarizes it, "Maurras's argument in *Le Romantisme féminin* is that the Romantic imagination is inherently feminine. It spawns self-absorption, perversity, emotional anarchy—the general attitude of, as he put it, a perpetual *'je souffre, donc je suis.'* To say that French culture was blighted by Romanticism was to say that it had been feminized" (1996, 37). Misogynistic discourse of integral nationalism became one of the many sources of its "rhetorical ambiguity" (Hanna 1994, 51), since the Action Française, while expressing contempt for femininity in general and for the choice of Marianne ("the slut") as the symbol of modern France in particular, found its own most cherished allegorical icon in the historical and mythic persona of another woman: the chaste and saintly Joan of Arc (Hanna 1985).[8]

These and other instances of the appropriation of metaphors of gender by discourses of national identity help foreground the crucial recognition that gender and nationality are akin in that they are both relational terms "whose identity derives from their inherence in a system of differences. In the same way that 'man' and 'woman' define themselves reciprocally . . . national identity is determined not on the basis of its own intrinsic properties, but as a function of what it (presumably) is not" (Parker et al. 1992, 5). For Maurras himself, the perniciously "feminine" nature of French Romanticism was directly attributable to the fact that its most prominent early figures—notably Rousseau and Mme de Staël—were foreigners bent on adulterating the native purity and virtue of the Gallic spirit. This symbiotic connection between the external and the internal other—the foreigner and the woman—was likewise operative in the negative view that Sardinha, as the principal ideologue and intellectual spokesman of Lusitanian Integralism, took of the *Lettres portugaises*'s undeservedly prominent role in the national literary canon. Countering with militant vehemence Teófilo Braga's enthusiastic endorsement of the work vis-a-vis the rest of national literary production in the seventeenth century, Sardinha accused his predecessor of being guided by a "pharisaic criterion of a Jacobin" and of professing patently false judgment over the "admirable [seventeenth] century—so Catholic, so classic, and so national!" (1929, 74–75). According to Sardinha, the letters became virtually homonymous with the misguided worldview promoted by what he labeled the Portuguese "ultra-Romanticism," or, as he described it, "the Portuguese synonym of the Romanticism that blew from France with the Revolution" (73–74).

Moreover though, in a bizarre doubling up of his historical argument, he actually held them responsible for the earlier emergence of that French Romantic sensibility in the first place: "It was precisely the fame of the *Lettres portugaises* that created [in the France of Louis XIV] that kind of psychological anomaly, engendering there a preromantic state of spirit" (101–2).

Given that the development of the argument briefly summarized above occupies over thirty pages of the essay Sardinha dedicated to the nun's letters, one could legitimately expect that the remaining nine would likely advocate their permanent expurgation from the national literary canon. That, however, is not the case. Indeed, in the last section of his article, Sardinha performs a curious roundabout. The passage is worth quoting in its entirety:

> Having restated the question in these terms, we discover that losing, with Soror Mariana, the aspect of a simple, particular case, the *Lettres* acquire a more comprehensive meaning. They express a general direction of taste and sensibility, which implicitly affirms a penetration (however illegitimate) of our lyricism into the classical and rigidly intellectual character of the France of Corneille and Racine. (105)

Sardinha then goes on to point out the similarly decisive influence of Jorge de Montemor's *Diana* on the French literary milieu of the time, and concludes:

> If we examine critically the genealogy outlined here, we will easily confirm the paternity, however spurious, of our lyricism with regard to the earliest Romantic effusions in France. It was one of the many ways by which Peninsularism contaminated the European community with the high splendor of its artistic and intellectual productions. (104–5)

Given the generally unwavering reliance of cultural nationalisms, in Portugal as elsewhere, on tropes of indisputable paternity, purity, and health of the nation, Sardinha's metaphors of "bastard penetration," "spurious paternity," and contamination appear curious indeed. And yet it is precisely from such a shakily ambiguous foundation that the proudly patriotic conclusion of his essay eventually arises, as he declares the *Lettres portugaises* "a document of spiritual influence exercised [by the Portuguese] in Europe" (113). Thus the distinctly "minor" qualities of Portuguese lyricism (in the sense theorized by Deleuze and Guattari) end up being co-opted by the major discourse of Portuguese nationalism. While such co-optation is a common enough phenomenon, as David Lloyd in particular has demonstrated in his writings on Irish literature, the ambivalent distinction bestowed on the *Lettres portugaises* by "major" discourses of national identity preserves and indeed emphasizes the necessarily self-contradictory nature of such an endeavor, beset by the "anxiety of canon formation" (Lloyd 1993, 5) that characterizes cultural nationalism.

The polemic regarding aesthetic and ideological significance of the Portuguese *seiscentismo* carried on for the better part of the decade, involving, on the other side of the battle lines, intellectuals connected with *Seara nova*, the journal whose founding in 1921 was explicitly conceived in order to "break the intellectual sway that the Integralists held over [Portuguese] youth" (Ramos 1994, 548). On the *Seara nova*'s side, the most prominent pronouncements on the issue came from the pen of António Sérgio, culminating in a 1926 lecture later published in the second volume of his *Ensaios*: "Cadaverous Kingdom, or the Cultural Question in Portugal" [O Reino Cadaveroso ou o problema da cultura em Portugal]. In the same vein as his opponents from *Nação Portuguesa*, Sérgio was eloquently blunt with regard to the ideological coordinates guiding his argument: the *seiscentismo* destroyed the splendid promise of Portuguese sixteenth-century secular humanism ("We move from the Kingdom of Intelligence to the Kingdom of Stupidity. . . . [T]he history of the country in the seventeenth century is a spectacle of emaciation of Portuguese mentality" [1972, 27]). Worse yet, its malignant legacy was said to continue to the present day: "Today,–we are as we were. . . . An authentic culture, a critical culture does not yet reign in Portugal. We are the 'Cadaverous Kingdom'; we are the Kingdom of Stupidity" (28).

Given the group's oppositional stance with regard to the Integralist movement, it is perhaps not much of a coincidence that two of *Seara nova*'s founders, Jaime Cortesão and Raul Proença, proved themselves admirers of Mariana and zealous defenders of the authenticity of her letters. Cortesão produced his own translation of the *Lettres portugaises* (1920) and argued passionately in favor of their national legitimacy and representative status: a strange and ill-fitting import into French literary canon, the letters must be appreciated in their natural, rightful setting of Portuguese tradition where they reveal multiple affinities with antecedents as remote as Galician-Portuguese love lyrics ("Certain phrases of our nun . . . already characterize national expression of tenderness in the earliest monuments of our lyric poetry" [17]). It was not enough to claim, according to Cortesão, that the letters belonged to the Portuguese literary treasury by virtue of having been written by a Portuguese woman; what assured them of canonical status was their timeless, archetypal quality of a collective national statement: "It is not just Mariana herself who signs them, it is the entire nation" (18).

Proença's contribution to the miscellany of *alcoforadista* discourse was more modest, but, given its context, no less significant. In the mid-1920s, the editor of *Seara nova* went on to direct one of the most ambitious publishing undertakings of the decade: the multivolume *Guia de Portugal*, which, in addition to the standard requirements of a practical tourist's manual, fulfilled a more exalted function of guiding native travelers on a voyage of discovery of their own country and on a pilgrimage to its most remarkable sites, "as if Portugal had become the Mecca of the Portuguese" (Ramos 1994, 585). Proença himself wrote the entry on Beja, placing Mariana Alcoforado among its other notable natives and dubbing her "the great amorous . . . eternal glory of the Portuguese sentiment" (148) and her letters "one of the most beautiful monuments of our literature" (150). Notwithstanding occasional challenges from the Integralist camp, the Portuguese Nun was by now widely and officially recognized as one of the glories (as well as one of premier tourist attractions) of her homeland, her letters a *pièce de résistance* of its literary canon.

Attacks at the notion of canonicity of the *Lettres portugaises* and at the exalted stature bestowed on their presumed author arrived however from other quarters as well, and as a result of quite different concerns and agendas. In 1915, José de Almada Negreiros, one of key figures of the Modernist vanguard, issued his celebrated *Manifesto Anti-Dantas*. Signed "José de Almada-Negreiros, Poeta d'*Orpheu*, Futurista e Tudo" (1993, 17), the manifesto was a viciously funny attack on the play *Soror Mariana*, written by Júlio Dantas, an immensely prolific and popular writer and a prominent member of the cultural establishment. Almada denounced the play, which was at the time enjoying considerable success at Lisbon's Ginásio Dramático, as a symptom of pervasive philistinism of Portuguese cultural mainstream, and an example of formulaic regurgitation of national tradition, whose icons were interchangeably offered up for public consumption: "Dantas made a Soror Mariana who could easily be a Soror Inês, or Inês de Castro, or Leonor Teles, or the Master of Aviz, or Dona Constança, or the Nau Catrineta, or Maria Rapaz!" (19)

Concluding a parodic summary of the play with a profane distortion of the heroine's name and obscenely insulting Dantas, whose homosexuality was a widely held secret ("that was not Marianna Alcoforado, but a Merdarianna Aldantascufurado"), Almada emphasized, however, that his goal was not an anarchic demolition of nationalist pieties, but rather a concerned defense of national dignity threatened by the complacent vulgarity of middle-class cultural tastes. It was because of the likes of Dantas that Portugal "[had] earned the reputation of the most backward country in Europe and in the whole world! The most savage country of all Africas! . . . A secluded Africa of the Europeans!" (23). Not unlike Sardinha and the Integralists, Almada combined a fervent dislike of Portuguese provincialism with a missionary desire to work for intellectual and artistic salvation of his homeland. As Manuel Villaverde Cabral points out, while the aesthetic traditionalism of the Integralist brand of cultural nationalism prevented the Modernists from associating with them, many points of contact may be detected between the two groups (1989, 23). Almada's other prominent manifesto, *Ultimatum futurista* (1917), made it clear that his objections were directed merely against the historicist bend of most nationalist writers, inadequate to the modern task of creating a new meaning for the *pátria* (Negreiros 1993, 37–43).

Notwithstanding the vocal minority of dissenters, the canonical standing of the *Cartas portuguesas* in the national literary and cultural treasury had been established and firmly cemented by the time serious challenges to their authenticity started to arrive, first from foreign, then also from local sources, the most prominent among the latter being A. Gonçalves Rodrigues's two articles, published in 1932 and 1935. In successive, revised editions of *História da Literatura Clássica* by Fidelino de Figueiredo, the section dedicated to Mariana Alcoforado and her love letters remains essentially unchanged from 1922 to 1946, although later editions offer, in a footnote, bibliographic updates which include recent, document-based challenges to the notion of Portuguese authenticity. Moreover, the popular appeal of that episode of national cultural history was such that Figueiredo was led to present his text in multiple reproductions. Prior to its inclusion in the volume, it had been published as an article in *Instituto* (Coimbra), from which a separate offprint was produced; and it was later read by the author as a public lecture in Real Gabinete Português de Leitura in Rio de Janeiro and reprinted there in the newspaper *Jornal do Comércio*.

Following the demise of Teófilo Braga, the five volumes of Figueiredo's *Histórias* became the leading compendium of Portuguese literary history; at the same time, however, the publishing market registered a proliferation of more or less comprehensive compendia, anthologies, and textbooks, reflecting increasing demand on the part of the literate population in general, and of the educational establishment in particular.[9] In a series of articles published in 1933 in the journal *Brotéria*, Paulo Durão registered this proliferation, while at the same time complaining bitterly about their generally poor quality and absence of guiding scholarly criteria:[10]

> Portuguese compilers of literature handbooks generally lack true scientific spirit, indispensable in any didactic work. This deficiency may be observed: in the criteria adopted for the appreciation of many works and authors; in lack of courage to react against certain unfounded, but still common bias; in neglecting to locate exact and complete information; in failing to reconcile newly obtained historical data with old analytic frameworks; in careless and unexamined acceptance of entirely arbitrary critical judgments. (160)

As a test case proving his negative diagnosis, Durão chose to examine sections of literary historical studies dealing with the letters of Soror Mariana, whose uncritical inclusion in (or equally uncritical exclusion from) the national canon the critic considered as one of leading outrages of Portuguese scholarship. Whether as defenders or detractors of the nun's authorship, Portuguese literary historians had demonstrated, according to Durão, sloppy laziness in failing to locate and cite relevant sources, and arbitrary flippancy in changing their minds on the question of authenticity without bothering to argue it properly one way or the other. Thus, once again, Mariana's love letters were given a richly symptomatic significance for the description of the national status quo. What's more, the critic's denunciation culminated in a warning against potentially adverse effects on his country's international reputation: as he argued, the doubtful measure of patriotic pride derived from the international prestige enjoyed by the *Lettres* was small compensation for the equally widespread disrepute that would surely befall Portuguese literary scholars who clung stubbornly to the discredited fiction of the nun's authorship (168).

Although Durão was able to note with satisfaction that the work had at least been withdrawn from the official list of readings for the classroom issued by the government, this development may be attributed less to any waning of popular interest in Soror Mariana than to a growing social and political conservatism imposed on the educational establishment by the incipient Estado Novo. As Sérgio Campos Matos notes, the 1930 curricular reform emphasized the objective of "moral development" as a guiding principle in the teaching of Portuguese literature, announcing expurgation of "all the texts whose content might lead to premature formation in the students of tendencies inappropriate at their age" (1990, 32). Given the atmosphere of Catholic revival under Salazar's dictatorship, love letters of a lapsed nun clearly belonged among such highly objectionable materials.

And yet, in spite of the removal of her letters from high school text-books, Mariana was hardly banished from the historical pantheon of celebrated heroines. In 1940, her portrait could be found on display in the main pavilion of the monumental Exposição do Mundo Português (Exhibition of the Portuguese World), where she was cataloged as a "great national figure" (Pereira 1941, 33). The exhibition, one of the most triumphant episodes of Salazar's dictatorship and an emblematic event of its "golden period" (Rosas 1994, 295), was designed, in the words of the exhibition's commissary general, as a "Symbolic City of Portuguese History" where, for the first time in the world, an entire civilization would be represented "in images and symbols" (Castro 1940, 55).[11] Nineteen-forty, the year of massive celebrations of the Double Centenary, encompassing both the tricentennial of the 1640 Restoration of Portuguese independence from Spain and the eighth centenary of Portugal's existence as an autonomous nation-state, also saw the publication of yet another "biography" of the nun. *Vida e morte de Madre Mariana* was penned by an Alentejan writer, Manuel Ribeiro, whose dedication made explicit the patriotic dimension of his project, the book being presented as

> The author's contribution to national commemorations of the Restoration of the *Pátria* and of the birth of Mother Mariana Alcoforado, glorious daughter of Beja and a great Heart, who carried throughout the World the name of Portugal and founded in the bronze of her *Cartas* an eternal memorial to Portuguese Sentiment. (v)

Conveniently born in the very year of the 1640 Restoration, an event considered by historians to constitute the first powerful manifestation of Portuguese nationality as a crucial superstructure of the Portuguese nation-state (Marques 1972–74, 436), the historical Mariana seemed destined to be cast as a national heroine, who, not unlike the Discoverers, "carried throughout the world the name of Portugal" and whose five brief love letters were now being newly unveiled as a monumental epitome of the national spirit, on equal footing—as Ribeiro very nearly postulated in his dedication—with such icons of Estado Novo's imperial ideology as the Padrão dos Descobrimentos (Monument of the Discoveries), also a remnant of the 1940 commemorations. Indeed, at least one reviewer accorded Ribeiro's vision of Mariana its rightful place in the "Symbolic City" of the exhibition by declaring that his book represented "a new and worthy pavilion in the admirable Exhibition of National Honor" (Monteiro 1941, 57).

MARIANA ALCOFORADO

*Painel de Jorge Barradas no pavilhão nobre
da Exposição do Mundo Português, 1940*

Mariana's figure as imagined by Jorge Barradas and displayed at the Exposição do Mundo Português.

Ribeiro himself had mentioned the presence of Mariana's likeness at the exhibition, among other "historic women of our land," commenting approvingly that "the *Pátria* would not be complete without her" (256). He too saw in her letters an internationally visible index of Portugueseness (comparable only to Camões), but viewed her notoriety as an entirely positive phenomenon: in fact, Mariana's letters were "highly Lusophile," in that the "tender sympathy that they have inspired in so many souls throughout the world . . . turns into an affection toward our homeland" (viii).

Vida e morte de Madre Mariana Alcoforado was reviewed by, among others, Alfredo Pimenta, who dedicated to Ribeiro's book an installment of his regular column in Lisbon's *Diário de Notícias*, under the banner "Portuguese Culture, Foreign Culture." Pimenta had already made more than one contribution to the polemic surrounding the letters, coming down firmly and repeatedly on the side of opponents of Portuguese authenticity.[12] He reaffirmed his stand in the present review, noting that Camões and Soror Mariana did in fact merit being mentioned in one breath, but for reasons different from those proposed by Ribeiro: theirs were the two cases in Portuguese literature that "[were] progressively being turned into victims of everybody's and anybody's fantasy and whim" (1941, 5). The reviewer also zeroed in on what was increasingly becoming the guiding feature of the *alcoforadista* discourse in Portugal: the divorce between fact and fiction, or history and myth. As a factual, historical occurrence, Portuguese authorship of the letters was indefensible; as a cultural fiction, it carried the irresistible appeal and explanatory power of grand mythic narratives. Ribeiro persisted in collapsing the two aspects, and therefore his book, while highly successful as a "romantic fantasy," was, according to Pimenta, ultimately a failed effort.

Another author, Leonardo Pereira, was sufficiently outraged by the inclusion of Soror Mariana in the pantheon of Portuguese femininity by the designers of the exhibition to pen an entire book of his own contesting the nun's undeserved prominence in her homeland. Accusing Mariana of "sadistic impudence" (1941, 30) and "mental pathology" (32), he painted an alternative portrait of "a pathetic woman who belongs in the gallery of Dostoevski's characters, sadly chained to a morbid love, mortified, useless and forsaken" (38). Interestingly, Pereira's comments on the Portuguese Nun's presence in the exhibition went beyond morality and into the realm of aesthetics, as he registered a strong objection to the late Modernist style of the painting, whose "strange design" (32) added further insult to his virtuous injury.[13]

Notwithstanding these and other challenges, Soror Mariana's mythic stature did not appear to be seriously affected. Other writers, paraphrasing Voltaire, had already suggested that if the Portuguese Nun had not existed, she would have had to be invented. As one prefacer wrote in 1925,

> Soror Mariana Alcoforado, given that she may not have existed and that her work may have been merely a literary hoax, would have entered the realm of reality, so extraordinary was the labor of fiction that succeeded in interpreting, through the formidable synthesis of the five letters, the feminine experience of a cloistered love. (Sequeira 1925, 9)

Likewise, where contemporary Portuguese critics and historians are virtually unanimous in accepting the *Lettres portugaises* as a literary fiction originating in France, many recent reenactments of Mariana's love story (including popular editions of the letters, exhibits, performances, and works of fiction) have taken for granted the prominent place claimed by the *Cartas portuguesas* in the cultural memory of their imaginary homeland and have dismissed, as accidental to their purpose, the issue of historically valid authorial authentication. A recent example of such a reorientation of interpretive preconditions and objectives could be found in a 1994 exhibition at the National Library in Lisbon entitled "Love in Portugal" and dedicated, in the words of Maria Leonor Machado de Sousa, to recalling "some amorous couples of particular significance in the Portuguese tradition" (1). Although the author of the brief introduction to the booklet published in conjunction with the exhibit conceded, in no uncertain terms, that the *Lettres portugaises* were "a forged text, with no possible reference to a real story," she nevertheless proceeded to justify the inclusion of Mariana and her French officer in the gallery of nationally celebrated lovers, couples both real and fictitious (we find there, among others, the historical figures of D. Pedro and Inês de Castro side by side with Carlos and Joaninha, the protagonists of Almeida Garrett's novel *Viagens na minha terra*), on the grounds of the international prominence gained by the letters along with their "paradigmatic view" of love *à la portugaise* (1). To judge from the list of paintings included in the exhibition, Mariana was in fact accorded a decidedly prominent place in its internal topography: no fewer than four original artworks depicted her and/or her lover, compared to two each dedicated to the runner-up couples, Pedro-Inês and Carlos-Joaninha. The divorce between the discourse of factual validation and the process of pop-cultural appropriation of national symbols, be they historic or fictional, has thus been proven complete.[14]

Looking back, it is easy to observe that much of the often heated debate between the *alcoforadistas* and the debunkers of Mariana's claim to the authorship of the *Lettres portugaises* has had as its implicit premise the desire to inscribe the text into a canonical formula of one sort or another. While the national canon of Portuguese literature has been the focus of this chapter, it is also possible to point to the genre-identified canon of European comparative literature with its "type portugais" (Jost); or to the author-identified canon of Guilleragues' literary works (Deloffre and Rougeot), which would hardly exist as such without the defining and distinguishing presence of the *Lettres portugaises*. However, Mariana's letters could in fact be seen as a radically non-canonical and non-canonizable work, deterritorialized and unlocatable to the highest degree, always slipping between discourses, languages, and cultures that attempt to claim it as their own, always registering a signifying surplus in excess of each and every one of those multiple claims. Perhaps only *Novas Cartas Portuguesas* (1972), the feminist manifesto collectively authored by Maria Isabel Barreno, Maria Teresa Horta, and Maria Velho da Costa, may be said to adequately represent that surplus through its own breathless excessiveness and uncontainable scope.

5

Gendering Mariana

MARIANA ALCOFORADO'S IDENTITY AS A WOMAN, AND, MORE SPECIFICALLY, as a woman writer, attracted far less attention in the first century of her celebrity in Portugal than her hotly affirmed or contested, and in either case much discussed, identity as Portuguese. In an early intervention, the novelist Camilo Castelo Branco, writing in his *Curso de Literatura Portuguesa* (1876), cited the notorious remark of Jean Jacques Rousseau ("I would bet everything I have that the *Lettres portugaises* were written by a man"), but, while similarly skeptical with regard to the letters' authenticity, chose to base his argument on culturally and historically specific differences in literary formation and taste between seventeenth-century Portugal and France, rather than on an "aesthetic of amorous endearments" determined by sexual difference (107). Camilo's contemporary, Teófilo Braga, who unwaveringly defended Mariana's authorship in his literary historical writings spanning four decades, likewise concentrated on what he felt to be the inherent Portugueseness of her amorous abandon, her letters constituting a documentary reflection of a disembodied *alma portuguesa*: an all-embracing distillation of the most authentic and representative characteristics of the race.

However, whether the "Portuguese soul" has ever in fact been construed as fully and neatly "disembodied" is a question wide open to debate. A point of departure may be found in the following remarks of Agostinho de Campos in his preface to Thereza Leitão de Barros's pioneering study of women's writing in Portugal, *Escritoras de Portugal* (1924):

> I will say . . . that the book *Escritoras de Portugal* has brought to my eyes, with renewed and forceful clarity, the following thesis: that Portuguese literature, essentially lyrical and, in its lyricism, essentially amorous. may be de-

scribed (although it was exercised almost exclusively by men until the beginning of this century) as a *feminine or womanly literature.* (Barros 9–10; original emphasis)

In spite of its evident hyperbole (apparently sensed by the author who hastened to qualify his excess by adding, somewhat contradictorily, "I am of course thinking of lyric poetry"), the above quote illustrates pointedly the claim advanced by the editors of a recent volume of essays exploring historically and culturally diverse relationships between "nationalisms and sexualities," with regard to the commonly encountered in Western cultural discourse "trope of the nation-as-woman": "If Britannia and Germania can . . . be gendered feminine, this iconography operates despite or rather *because* of the actual experiences of their female populations," women being "subsumed only symbolically into the national body politic" (Parker et al. 1992, 6; original emphasis). A similar compromise appeared to structure, for Campos and others, what may be termed as the national body politic of Portuguese literature, which could be imagined as feminine despite—or perhaps, indeed, because—of the fact that it had been "exercised" almost exclusively by men.

In addition, however, Campos's suggestion provides a convenient articulation of one of the most pervasive cultural stereotypes participating in the makeup of Portuguese national identity: involving both genre and gender, it blends what Jacinto do Prado Coelho called the nation's "already proverbial inclination toward the lyric" (1977, 40) with a usually less explicit, but just as common, attribution of personality traits traditionally identified in the West as feminine: gentleness, passivity, contemplative and affectionate disposition, dislike of violent and extreme measures. Such an attribution becomes particularly clear when, as often happens, Portugal is contrasted with Spain: as Fidelino de Figueiredo put it in an epigrammatic encapsulation of the cliché, "if Spanish literature is force, Portuguese literature is love, erotic intrigue, lyricism, subjectivity, contemplation, daydreaming, and nostalgia; and when it expresses force, it does so under an appeasing influence of lyricism" (quoted in Coelho 1977, 41). It has been noted how this contrastive valorization of Lusitanian identity was once employed toward an exculpation of Portuguese colonial expansion overseas, with its most elaborate ideological formulation in Gilberto Freyre's anthropological doctrine of Luso-Tropicalism. To quote another self-proclaimed mythographer of the national soul, "where Spaniards were conquerors, we were colonizers. . . . While a natural Franciscanism impelled us to love people and things of the world we had uncovered, the

Spaniard was driven to subjugate, in a Dominican manner, all that differed from himself" (Oliveira 1947, 22).

Full-scale archaeological investigation of such a rich and elaborate cultural mythology is obviously beyond the scope of this study; it is worth noting, however, that it provided a fertile ground and a bottomless source of justification for Portuguese reappropriation of the *Lettres portugaises* as a nationally representative text and for the imagining of their author's real-life persona in a perfect homology between Mariana's body, her letters, and the deepest essence of the national spirit. For Teófilo Braga, Mariana's passionate soul, at the same time *raison d'être* of the letters and the unshakable attestation of their national authenticity, became an indispensable cornerstone in the construction, from inside out, as it were, of her physical and psychological identity. It was because of her truly Portuguese nature that the teenage nun could achieve such maturity of expression in her amorous abandon: according to Teófilo, that nature was in fact the true author of the letters, which, "dictated by a Peninsular temper, convey the passion of a thirty-year-old" (1870, 189).[1] If Mariana is all soul (elsewhere she is called "a pure soul, thirsting for light" [194]), her French lover Chamilly is, by contrast, all body, endowed with "a robust constitution" (190), and whose "animal nature compelled him to follow blindly the scent of the flesh" (201). This antithetical relationship between the two is likewise projected onto the body of the text: while the French words constitute its physical reality, its Portuguese "sentiment" unmistakably shines through the material layer: "The Portuguese soul impressed upon the sentiment [of the letters] a form all of its own, which the French words could not obliterate" (211).

The conflation of Mariana's body with the body of her text, along with the attendant casting of this hybrid *corpus* in a specifically national mold, was to become a frequent theme in subsequent Portuguese interpretations of the letters. Writing over fifty years after Teófilo, Afonso Lopes Vieira imagined the nun's five epistles as "five endless kisses that unfold into five endless sobs" (1922, 258) and, summing up his critique of existing Portuguese translations, or "versions," of the text, likened them to instruments of torture inflicted upon its, as well as Mariana's, vulnerable body. Exuberant feats of fancy directed at imagining Mariana's physical and psychological identity, and in particular of her unmistakably female, and often highly sexualized body, fill the repository of *alcoforadista* discourse with much purple prose bordering on soft core pornography. To offer just one fairly representative example, here is a writer waxing prurient on the subject of Mariana's pubescent self prematurely imprisoned in her monastic closure: "Her gentle body was developing, bursting with life and straining against the barely supported torture of the hair shirt. The atmosphere of mysticism . . . excited her senses" (Guimarães, 2).

Coincidentally, the heyday of the Portuguese Nun's popularity in her native country overlapped with a pervasive vogue enjoyed, among Portuguese intellectuals in the first decades of the twentieth century, by the ideas of the French philosopher Henri Louis Bergson (Ramos 1994, 529–30). Bergson's concept of *élan vital*, a vital impetus that drove life against, and in spite of, limitations and mortality inherent in matter, offered a promising opportunity for Portuguese *alcoforadistas* seeking to dramatize the contrast between the exuberance of Soror Mariana's passion and the many, literal as well as figurative, obstacles imposed on her by overwhelming forces of external circumstance.[2] Writing in 1912, Manuel Ribeiro was explicit in his Bergsonian leanings when he imagined Mariana as "a woman [who was] physically and spiritually healthy" (17) and who struggled against the limitations of her monastic existence:

> Mariana . . . was surely one of those strong creatures made to live a full life and to feel love . . . that human love, vital and fecund, that throbs in the flesh and bears fruit in sweet delights of motherhood. . . . Her *élan vital* . . . saved her from succumbing to mystical raptures and passional perversions that are provoked by the monotony of the cloister. (14–15)

Other writers, however, would take the opposite course, choosing instead to inscribe Mariana's story with evidence of perversion and pathology. The most remarkable effort of that kind was carried out by Asdrúbal de Aguiar, a professor of legal medicine and a pioneering practitioner of "sexual science" in Portugal, in which capacity he authored many works on such topics as male and female homosexuality, hysteria, rape, and incest. Aguiar's writings combined an avowed adoption of a morally disinterested perspective with effective denunciation of sexual phenomena he described, with particular emphasis on homosexuality, as anomalous and closely related to criminal behavior (Ramos 1994, 664–65). Another fertile line of inquiry developed by the sexologist resulted in several studies dedicated to alleged cases of sexual pathology found in the annals of Portuguese history, particularly among the members of royal families. One such "medical-psychological study" diagnosed the king D. Fernando I as a "true masochist" and his wife D. Leonor Teles as a "legitimate example of sadism" (1924, 186–87).[3] Aguiar adopted a similar analytic angle in his study of Soror Mariana Alcoforado; as he declared in his introduction, he planned to

attempt to discover in the admirable words of the five letters . . . evidence of
moral masochism suffered by the famed religious, proof of the coarsest of
pleasures that she experienced when confronted with ruthless and insensi-
tive behavior of the man whom she so passionately loved. (1922, 6)

Abundantly annotated with references to such works as Kraft-Ebbing's
Psychopatia sexualis and Eulenburg's *Sadismus und Masochismus*,
Aguiar's book pictured Mariana as a character straight out of Sacher-
Masoch, going as far as to juxtapose a number of quotations excerpted
from the Austrian author's writings with analogous declarations found in
the text of the *Lettres portugaises* (83–84).[4] Far from contenting himself
with such a one-dimensional diagnosis, however, Aguiar threw in a couple
of other "perversions" he claimed to have detected in Mariana's letters,
following up on his assertion that perverted individuals tended to display
symptoms of several anomalous psychic syndromes ("And so we have
sadists who are at the same time necrophiliacs or exhibitionists, there are
exhibitionists who are also given to bestiality, there are homosexuals who
are not adverse to fetishism, etc") (89). Thus, as he argued, the haughtiness
displayed in Mariana's final letter to Chamilly might indicate a slight tendency toward sadism, while her first missive contained a passage that
alluded to a possible fetishistic attitude toward her lover. Aguiar's concluding claim related the nun's "permanent neuropathological condition"
to her antecedents and successors in the genealogical narrative of the
Alcoforado family, with particular emphasis on its eventual extinction
through incest and mental degeneration (117–18; see chapter 2 for an
account of the history of the Alcoforados).

Notwithstanding the interest in Mariana's femininity, which, after a
slow start in the early stages of her fame, was increasingly attracting attention of her Portuguese commentators, it is relatively rare to find in the
avalanche of *alcoforadista* writings significant contributions by women
authors. In fact, as late as 1941, Alfredo Pimenta could still note that only
men had "studied, dissected, scrutinized the case of Maria Ana [sic],"
going on to recommend that an end finally be put to "all this comedy" and
to observe rather sensibly: "how can we, sturdy specimens of the male sex,
obtain sufficient understanding of female psychology to disguise ourselves
as Maria Ana Alcoforado and attempt to interpret feelings of a seventeenth-
century woman" (5). Driven by his demystificatory agenda, Pimenta had
no reason to dwell on well-established Portuguese antecedents of such literary or interpretive "disguise," from medieval Galician-Portuguese lyric
to the curious case of the poet Violante de Cysneiros invented by the

all-male Modernist *Orpheu* circle.[5] In addition, the critic exaggerated somewhat in his claim: the most prominent Portuguese female intellectual of the late nineteenth and early twentieth century, the first woman to be admitted to the Lisbon Academy of Sciences, Maria Amália Vaz de Carvalho, had dedicated two essays to the Portuguese Nun and in one of her pieces compared Mariana's letters to the epistolary writings of Mlle de Léspinasse and George Sand.[6] Furthermore, in 1924, Thereza Leitão de Barros accorded Mariana Alcoforado a prominent place in her comprehensive study of *Escritoras de Portugal*. It was not until 1944, however, with the publication of Alice de Oliveira's *Vida amorosa de Soror Mariana*, that Pimenta's implicit postulate was fulfilled by this novelistic biography, rich in psychological musings, produced by a woman author intent on celebrating "one of the few Portuguese women whom the world has declared famous" (80). Significantly, it is her heroine's writing skills, demonstrated from an early age, that are highlighted in Oliveira's "reconstitution" of the nun's life: the studious and intellectually curious young Mariana is shown as "always attentive to matters of the mind, buried among books and busy transcribing, in her very awkward handwriting, some text that has awakened her interest" (22).

It is precisely this habit, unusual and undesirable in a girl, that irks Mariana's father and leads him to conceive the idea of shutting her in a convent, where she soon becomes the scribe's assistant and eventually the scribe herself: "Soror Mariana had become definitively the scribe of the Mosteiro [sic] da Conceição, since no one surpassed her in her talent for organizing and in the swiftness with which she could execute any writing task" (46).

In an instance of ironic justice, Mariana's ultimate writing accomplishment in the end becomes the instrument of her father's punishment: he dies of a stroke after having received in the mail an anonymously sent copy of the published *Lettres portugaises*. Mariana's brother and heir to the family fortune (from which his sister was excluded upon being forced into the convent) also suffers a proper, if less severe, penalty, becoming a monk himself in shame over Mariana's disgrace made public.

The emphasis placed by Oliveira on the activity of writing as a focal aspect of Mariana's identity had not been a common ingredient in the stock repertoire of the *alcoforadista* discourse. It is therefore particularly important to stress that the Portuguese Nun's mythic prominence in her native country could only be assured, paradoxically, by protestations of her historical reality not merely as a Portuguese and a woman, but, specifically, as a Portuguese woman *writer*. In other words, Mariana Alcoforado

the provincial nun who allowed herself to be seduced by a dashing Frenchman, thereby providing fodder for tales of his exotic amorous exploits and,
eventually, for an ingenious writer's literary imagination, did not offer a
particularly promising basis for an exercise of nationalist vanity; Mariana
Alcoforado the epistolary genius who translated her fiery peninsular passion into rhetorical cadences worthy of the greatest masters of *le grand
siècle* was another matter altogether. At the same time, although the characterization of Mariana as a talented and accomplished writer would
appear to make her a virtual homologue of such unquestionably real seventeenth-century female literary figures as (among others) Violante do
Céu, Maria do Céu, and Madalena da Glória, all of whom were nuns as
well as celebrated Baroque poets, the instances of a similar parallel being
traced are strikingly rare in the voluminous body of interpretive writing
surrounding Mariana as the presumed author of the *Lettres portugaises*.
What more, when they have occurred, it was as likely as not for the purpose of establishing a contrast rather than a likeness; thus, for example, the
author of the preface to a 1914 Portuguese edition of the text drew a firm
distinction separating the notorious nun from the few women writers who,
at that time, could be said to belong to the national historical literary
canon: "Mariana, who was not in fact an educated writer, unlike Luiza
Sijeia [sic], Paula Vicente or the marquise d'Alorna, [figures] in the history of Portuguese literature with a name whose brilliance overshadows
the names of those illustrious women" (Gomes, 19–20).

If, as a female writer, Mariana was thus presented as towering over both
her predecessors and her descendants in the imaginary lineage of Portuguese literary women, as a woman pure and simple she likewise lent herself to demagogic recasting that, at least in one striking example, set her
apart from and against her twentieth-century Portuguese sisters. In a 1913
public lecture entitled "Soror Mariana" and later serially published in the
newspaper *O Dia*, the speaker, one António Guimarães, having rhap-
sodized for some time about the nun as an exemplary bearer of a "Portuguese woman's heart" and "an eloquent source of pride for the
Portuguese woman," launched an odd and unforeseeable attack on his contemporary suffragettes, qualifying as "foolish" their goal of "the liberation
of women through social demands" and going on to thunder against this
"caricature of a woman,"

> the political woman of our time, this absurd little monster that shouts at ral-
> lies, manufactures explosives and protests in public squares; and who, almost
> as a general rule, seems to have obtained exclusive rights to ugliness. . . .

This analysis may perhaps seem a little harsh . . . ; but I find it repugnant to believe that inside such a creature, who spends all day in the streets demanding the right to vote, to intervene in the country's political mechanism, might exist all the subtleties of a woman's soul.

By the time Guimarães delivered his lecture, Soror Mariana was well on her way to becoming all things to all people. Molding the significance of her life, love, body, and writing to whatever shape would seem most appropriate in a given ideological context has been a constant feature of the *alcoforadista* discourse ever since Morgado de Mateus rescued the Portuguese text of the *Lettres portugaises* from its unauthentic Frenchness just a few years after Napoleon's troops had ravaged Portugal amassing prodigious spoils of war that (as wistfully noted by the historian Oliveira Marques) can still be found today in French museums and libraries (1972–74, 578). However, discursive gendering of the Portuguese Nun in her native country, in contrast to the many instances of such discourse produced on the international scene, has been burdened by unique and uniquely complex challenges. In particular, the possibility of situating Soror Mariana Alcoforado and her celebrated love letters within a hypothetical genealogy of Portuguese women's writing presents a fundamental difficulty that may be summed up as follows: the most acclaimed, both nationally and internationally (at least until mid-twentieth century), Portuguese woman writer was most likely neither Portuguese nor a woman. Nevertheless, it is both possible and illuminating to examine the sometimes uneasy and often contradictory critical and artistic efforts to integrate the figure of Mariana Alcoforado within such a putative lineage, efforts complicated in more recent times by the problematic issue of treating an author whose historical authenticity is at best highly doubtful as a potentially real literary foremother.

Such doubts and contradictions did not concern Thereza Leitão de Barros, the author of *Escritoras de Portugal*, a study subtitled "Feminine Genius Revealed in Portuguese Literature," published in Lisbon in 1924. While Barros subscribed to the dominant consensus regarding the letters' authenticity, her treatment of the "Flower of Portugal," as she nicknamed Soror Mariana, in spite of its celebratory register was hardly free from ambiguity, in fact foreshadowing already the dilemmas and solutions present in some of the later, more self-consciously problematized attempts at placing the controversial author of the *Lettres portugaises* within the narrative structure of national literary history. The brief chapter dedicated to the prodigious nun provides a closure for the first volume of Barros's opus; the critic comments on both the chapter's brevity and its importance, indicating that this segment of her work is simultaneously "the smallest and the greatest" among the book's components (207). She also remarks, albeit indirectly, upon its strategic positioning: it is presented as both an apotheotic culmination and an antithetical questioning of what Barros has discussed in the preceding chapters; namely, the work of seventeenth-century, for the most part cloister-bound, women writers to whom she refers as a "grey crowd of literary nuns" (201) and whose sheer numbers allow her to characterize the period as something of a heyday for female intellectual creativity, surpassing in that respect even Barros's own twentieth-century setting (191). Nevertheless, it is with an "exhausted pen" (212) that Barros concludes registering lives and works of that "endless procession of Portuguese women who, in the course of one century, kept brightly aflame their dedication to education and writing" (201), in order to turn finally to her truly beloved heroine whom she imagines standing proudly and defiantly alone on her "tall and isolated pillar of glory" (201). Thus, in spite of the pioneering design and scope of her protofeminist work, by treating Mariana Alcoforado not only as one of the number of "escritoras de Portugal," but also, at the same time, as their unequaled superior, Barros unwittingly aligned with some of her decidedly nonfeminist predecessors and contemporaries in subscribing to a sort of historical literary tokenism traditionally practiced, in Portugal as elsewhere, with regard to outstanding female artists and intellectuals.

In the particular case of Soror Mariana, such practice led of course directly into the deeply ironic dilemma of privileging a figure whose legitimate standing on grounds of not only nationality but also gender would in the end prove largely indefensible. The most sophisticated and suggestive attempt to account for the significance of the misattribution of the author's gendered identity within the framework of Portuguese literary history, as well as in the putative context of a yet-to-be-written "herstory" of Portuguese women, is due to Luciana Stegagno Picchio in her brief, but richly textured "Note sulla letteratura femminile in Portogallo," an essay introducing an anthology of contemporary Portuguese women poets published in Italy (1980). Stegagno Picchio titles her preface "Le nipoti di Marianna," Mariana's granddaughters; the title serves to underscore the critic's point that "for centuries, feminine literature in Portugal was what male writers . . . imagined it would be like if Portuguese women of letters were not women and therefore, by constitution and definition, incapable of literature" (6–7). The Italian scholar refers here to the long tradition of *sui generis* literary transvestitism that has permeated Portuguese cultural history since the Medieval *cantigas de amigo*, imitations of women's songs authored by male poets and therefore, according to Stegagno Picchio, examples of "anthropomorphic fantasy" akin to such other fabulous vehicles of otherness as Aesop's animals or James Fenimore Cooper's romanticized American Indians (7). The critic's tongue-in-cheek choice of Soror Mariana as the literary foremother presiding over the assembly of modern Portuguese women writers becomes therefore aptly and meaningfully symptomatic of the full spectrum of ironic ambivalence surrounding the issues of gendered subjectivity and authorship in Portuguese literature, beginning with its historical and symbolic inception in the country's earliest recorded examples of artistic discourse.

Another point made by Stegagno Picchio with regard to the difficulties inherent in the task of tracing a symbolic genealogy of Portuguese women's writing (and in that she echoes and has been echoed by many others) has to do with the undeniable scarcity of plausible role models among the female writers recorded, however marginally, by national literary history. Thereza Leitão de Barros already intimated as much when, while urging "educated Portuguese women of today" (192) to pay respectful attention to the lives and works of their intellectual precursors, she also repeatedly complained about the inability of her subjects (with the sole exception of Soror Mariana) to inspire her unconditional admiration. Stegagno Picchio's verdict is therefore that, given the unreliability of both historical and mythical or symbolic foundations that an autonomous tradition of women's writing in Portugal might claim as its own, attempting to establish a "rigorously feminine genealogy" in Portuguese letters presents itself as an absurd task [rendendo assurda una loro genealogia rigorosamente femminile] (7). "Mariana's granddaughters," contemporary Portuguese women writers, remain therefore motherless, as it were, even while they reclaim their rightful place in the national literary canon.[7]

Where Thereza Leitão de Barros, in her early twentieth-century account of female literary tradition in Portugal, accorded Soror Mariana a prominent and obfuscating presence, in the Italian critic's essay, written fifty-five years later, the nun's name figures instead as an equivocal and elusive—if also prominently displayed—index of an absence. A similar ambivalence, although less suggestively explored, characterizes the brief mention of the *Lettres portugaises* in Isabel Allegro de Magalhães's *O Tempo das Mulheres*, a study of contemporary Portuguese women's fiction whose substantial portion is dedicated however to tracing "antecedents of the place occupied by women in Portuguese literature today" (1987, 103). If available historical and textual evidence did not point overwhelmingly in the direction of Guilleragues's (French male) authorship, the author states, the letters would necessarily occupy a central place within her presentation; as it is, they can only be mentioned in passing (152). Here, once again, Mariana's presence is evoked primarily in order to signify her absence: an empty center left unclaimed by any presumptive heiress or usurper of her celebrity.

The Portuguese Nun's historical elusiveness has not, however, acted as a deterrent to the editors of an anthology of critical essays on contemporary Portuguese women's writing recently published in Germany under the title *Die Schwestern der Mariana Alcoforado [The Sisters of Mariana Alcoforado]*. In their introduction, Elfriede Engelmeyer and Renate Hess comment on the irony inherent in the historically established tradition of privileging the mythic figure of Mariana Alcoforado over the undeniably real writing nuns of the Portuguese Baroque, who, according to the editors, only recently have begun to be discovered and acknowledged, and therefore "cannot really be regarded as forerunners of contemporary women's writing" (1993, 7).[8] In choosing to collectively label the authors represented in their anthology as the sisters, rather than the granddaughters, of Mariana Alcoforado, Engelmeyer and Hess make implicit what they go on to spell out in their introduction: that their primary reference is less the epistolary output of the Portuguese Nun herself than its most prominent, as well as the most radical, modern remake: the *Novas Cartas Portuguesas* by Maria Isabel Barreno, Maria Teresa Horta, and Maria Velho da Costa. Since the German editors view the publication of *Novas Cartas* as "both the concrete and symbolic starting point of a very rich female-authored literature" that exists in contemporary Portugal, the title chosen for their anthology "contains a reference to the reinterpretation of Mariana, and to her quest for identity through writing" that are central themes of *Novas Cartas*. More significantly, it also points to "the sense of sisterhood" proclaimed in that work, a sense Engelmeyer and Hess wish to reclaim as an agent binding together, in spite of their differences, the Portuguese women writers of today (7–8). In so doing they distance themselves (however implicitly) from Stegagno Picchio's more skeptical and ironic view with regard to genealogical deployability of Mariana Alcoforado as a protofeminist writing foremother.

Barreno, Horta, and Velho da Costa, the self-constituted writing collective who in the early 1970s undertook to once again retell Mariana's story, faced a task made difficult by circumstances far exceeding the inherent complications of the myth. A short few years before the publication of *Novas Cartas*, Álvaro Manuel Machado, reviewing four Portuguese novels recently translated into French for the Parisian magazine *La Quin-*

zaine littéraire, had commented on "the difficulty of being Portuguese" as a common theme revealed in the novels. For the critic, this difficulty consisted in the compulsion to regard the nation's future from a temporally anomalous perspective, determined by a sense of history remaining frozen in time: "because in Portugal history stopped long ago, because it is no longer but myth and dilettantism" (12). The writing, publication (in 1972), and subsequent banning of *Novas Cartas* by the Portuguese regime demonstrated forcefully how the stagnant waters of social and political reality under Salazar's dictatorship and his successor Marcelo Caetano's only superficially more liberal rule made it particularly difficult to be Portuguese while also being a woman and a courageously transgressive writer to boot. Portuguese history was soon to become awakened from its dormancy by the 1974 military coup and the Revolution of Carnations that followed in its wake; likewise, the dormant myth of Soror Mariana was jolted from its clichéd, canonical status by the three writers' radical retelling of her story.

Barreno, Horta, and Velho da Costa discovered in the story of the Portuguese Nun an apparently inexhaustible repository of sources for their leading goal, a survey of patterns both mythic and factual, contemporary as well as historical, that have shaped Portuguese women's lives and works. The tribulations suffered by the authors, who were taken to court by the Caetano regime on charges of, among others, "outrage to public decency," have been comprehensively described (Sadlier 1989, 6–7). It has also been noted that widespread international prominence of *Novas Cartas* considerably surpassed both the degree of projection attained (by the mid-seventies at least) by any other twentieth-century work of Portuguese literature, and the impact the book exercised on the national cultural and literary scene, in spite of the publicity generated by the trial. It is instructive, in this context, to note that a perusal of Portugal's preeminent literary journal, *Colóquio/Letras*, and in particular of its regular section dedicated to current "literary information" for the years 1972–75, yields just two mentions of *Novas Cartas*; that both appear under the heading "Portuguese literature abroad"; and that the first one, in the November 1974 issue, is a report on two Portuguese items featured in a recent issue of the Parisian *Quinzaine littéraire*, one of them being the review, by Claudine Herrmann, of the just-released French translation of the book. This contemporary mirroring of the original "reexportation from France" of Mariana's letters may be seen as yet another, peculiar instance of the syndrome of "asymmetric communication" (Lourenço 1983) between Portugal and France or, more broadly, Portugal and "Europe," especially if we observe that at the time of the book's original publication only one review had appeared in any of Lisbon's major newspapers. Interestingly, the reviewer, Nuno de Sampayo, in spite of his enthusiastic appraisal of *Novas Cartas*, was somewhat pessimistic with regard to its potential international projection, an attitude that may be illuminated by the mention of another journalistic intervention, which appeared in the same month of May 1972 in the daily *Diário Popular*. The newspaper was at the time publishing a series of responses from leading Portuguese (and in one case German) writers and critics to the question it had posed to them: "What are the causes of foreign ignorance with regard to Portuguese literature?" According to an already familiar pattern, the *inquérito* was conceived as a reaction to a recent issue of the French weekly *Le Nouvel Observateur* dedicated to foreign (non-French) literatures, in which no mention at all was made of Portuguese letters.[9] Once again, the peripheral compulsion to view one's own culture through foreign eyes colluded with another symptom of geocultural marginality, an exacerbated resentment experienced whenever the privileged foreign gaze fails to include one's particular section of the periphery in its sweeping field of outbound vision. It is no wonder therefore that, shortly thereafter, the records of the trial stood by the "Three Marias" (as the authors of *Novas Cartas* had come to be nicknamed) would abound in arguments evoking a similar framework of central-peripheral interaction, albeit in this case prompted by the uncommon phenomenon of close and intense focus that foreign observers directed toward Portugal at the time of the trial.

Full documentation of the court proceedings was gathered and published (in 1974) by Duarte Vidal, the lawyer for the defense retained by Maria Isabel Barreno. This invaluable resource contains, among other materials, depositions by many prominent Portuguese intellectuals who on numerous occasions referred to the international projection attained by *Novas Cartas* and to the attention the international press was paying to the persecution suffered by the book's authors. Barreno herself commented, in her official testimony, on the "great interest" that the book had aroused in "intellectual circles of the civilized world," thus becoming a "work that honors Portuguese letters and has already crossed . . . national borders" (34). Natália Correia expressed her confidence that the book was going to be translated into many more languages, "which will promote the most widespread propagation that Portuguese literature has seen in many years" (38). Urbano Tavares Rodrigues referred to French, Brazilian, and Spanish writers he had personally consulted on the matter, and whose responses convinced him that "*Novas Cartas Portuguesas* contributed toward a most honorable projection of Portuguese literature throughout the civilized world" (40). Further depositions from Augusto Abelaira, José Tengarrinha, and Maria Lamas, among others, sounded a similar note, pointing to the contrast between the book's enthusiastic reception abroad and its vilification by the Portuguese authorities. On 4 April, shortly before the originally scheduled sentencing date, Barreno's attorney further dramatized the discrepancy in his summation (72–74):

> And therefore the book is going to be translated in more than ten countries and only here, in Portugal, it is considered pornographic and offensive to public morality? Can we really allow this to happen without inflicting great offense and disgrace on our own country and giving an official stamp of approval to the notion that we continue to be, as they called us in the seventeenth century, the "Kaffirs of Europe"? . . . This is a book that honors Portuguese literature and is giving it great projection abroad, a phenomenon in which all Portuguese should take pride. . . . Never, before today, had a work of Portuguese literature provoked such curiosity in the entire world and awakened such interest as this one. It is a public, well-known fact, and even here, in this court, it is confirmed by the great number of foreign journalists and television cameras in attendance. (72–74)

While the immediate international prominence achieved by *Novas Cartas* may be seen as mirroring, *mutatis mutandis*, the rapid internationalization of its seventeenth-century intertextual antecedent, I would argue that the revolutionary thrust of *Novas Cartas* depended less on the book's universal appeal, and therefore universal translatability and exportability across national borders, than on its profound and complex engagement with the specificity of its Portuguese cultural and political context. As Hélder Macedo wrote, reviewing the English translation of *Novas Cartas* for *Times Literary Supplement*, the text needs to be situated in this specificity both synchronically (that is, "in the context of the broad and long-standing anti-fascist struggle" in Portugal) and diachronically, with regard to what Macedo termed "the old tradition of Portuguese feminist literature" (1975, 1484). Although it would be difficult to qualify as "feminist" the majority of texts constituting the Portuguese tradition of mythifying Soror Mariana's life, love, and writing, it is also in the context of that tradition, with all of its multiple excesses and contradictions, that *Novas Cartas Portuguesas* should be read: as a politically self-conscious reclaiming, in the guise of what Roland Barthes called "an experimental myth, a second-order myth" (1987, 135), of a cultural fiction that was both crucially influential and, at the same time, highly malleable and therefore susceptible to ideological manipulation.

The dialectic of deterritorialization and reterritorialization, which from the early nineteenth century informed the enterprise of national reappropriation of the *Lettres portugaises*, was once again set in motion by the publication of *Novas Cartas*. As Macedo remarked in his review, the book was internationally promoted "as a generic and easily marketable commodity . . . a feminist, or rather anti-male manifesto disconnected from its political context" (1484). Thus denationalized, *Novas Cartas Portuguesas* came close to becoming yet another "Portuguese fiction," along with its own famous precedent and pretext or with Barrett Browning's *Sonnets from the Portuguese*. What distinguished this particular instance was the fact that the book was also politically co-opted—or reterritorialized in the international context—by the women's liberation movements of the early seventies and beyond, particularly in the United States. To cite but one example, in a voluminous compendium of the international women's movement, *Sisterhood Is Global* (published in 1984 and therefore well after the heyday of the book's popularity), the reference to *Novas Cartas* was still given a prominent status within the essay on Portugal by Maria de Lurdes Pintasilgo (Morgan, 571–75). In a subtle move of resistance against this powerful tide of appropriation, Macedo chose to "relusify" *Novas Cartas*, as it were, emphasizing the text's indebtedness to Portuguese cultural and literary tradition. Further, by titling his review "Teresa and Fátima and Isabel" (in an implicit but powerful contrast to the title of the book's English translation), Macedo dehomogenized the collective, culturally stereotyped, fiction of the "Three Marias," emphasizing the particular and the distinct over generic cohesion of commodified identity.

By repeating the already traditional gesture of reappropriating Mariana Alcoforado in order to graft her onto the contemporary Portuguese ground, "Teresa and Fátima and Isabel," acutely aware of the threat "to be the same thing in another form" (1994, 108), sought to transform the myth from within, as they combined an affirmation of its liberating potential with a subversion of its repressive implications in their unique exploration and questioning of the double bind of gender and nationality that has historically structured the Portuguese Nun's identity in the (real) country of her (fictional) origin.[10] *Novas Cartas* never actually addresses the question of Soror Mariana's authenticity: as the authors make clear in their groundbreaking work, the nun's fictional status in no way diminishes the potential of her story to supply a basis for a meaningful and politically effective analysis of the historical and contemporary predicament of real Portuguese women. On the contrary, it frees them to play loose, on a number of occasions, with that story's more or less established version. Nevertheless, the book remains quite closely attuned to its seventeenth-century pretext, incorporating several instances of rigorously parallel rewriting: among the earliest and most significant ones is the opening apostrophe of the "Third Letter I"—"Consider, my sisters . . ." (16)—a direct paraphrase of the notorious initial invocation of the *Lettres portugaises*, "Considère, mon amour. . . ." As this address indicates, the circuit of communication generated in *Novas Cartas* presents itself as a radical reorientation of its precedent and, by fully intentional extension, of the entire cultural and sociopolitical context in which literary communication takes place. In lieu of a solitary woman writer addressing an absent male reader (or, as an alternative reading of the apostrophe would have it, narcissistically invoking her own passion), a female community stages a communicational event in which the roles of speakers and addressees are shared and freely exchanged, circulating in an open-ended process of a textual give-and-take. The fundamental feminist premise of experiential commonality and consequent political solidarity among women is thus not merely a leading theme in *Novas Cartas*: as Maria de Lurdes Pintasilgo has observed, it also underlies the book's originative design and its resulting structure (1982, 11–12). In terms of speech act theory, the manifesto of sisterhood in *Novas Cartas* is both constative and performative: its words speak of actions which, in the act of speaking, they also perform.

In their exploration of historical and contemporary, as well as actual and potential, aspects of Portuguese women's condition, the authors of *Novas Cartas* make constant use of what Helena Michie has termed "the grammar of the family" (1992, 1). As Michie points out, "feminism has come to occupy a contradictory place with regard to the family," at the same time decrying it as the ground on which women's oppression by the society is most visibly and pervasively enacted and "reclaim[ing] the family" by "reproduc[ing] it in altered form"; feminist critique of the family "comes from within the family, and from within the structuring metaphor that makes intimacy the place of conflict" (1). The dominant familial tropes of feminist theory and practice, which at the same time structure the feminist project along its complementary diachronic and synchronic axes, are of course motherhood and sisterhood: "No matter how problematized, metaphors of sisterhood and motherhood remain central to the feminist project. 'Sister' and 'mother' become the vessels that contain, shape and delimit feminist discourse just as the family as it is now construed contains and shapes the roles and bodies of 'real' mothers and sisters" (2).

In *Novas Cartas Portuguesas* the metaphorics of the family is abundantly deployed; it is particularly interesting to observe how it is applied in the process of articulating a tentative intellectual genealogy of Portuguese women, inclusive of, but not limited to, Portuguese women writers, a genealogy in which Soror Mariana Alcoforado remains a central if not unproblematic figure, an icon centrally decentered, as it were, whose meanings constantly shift and multiply, even as it continues to retain its exemplary status. The need for establishing such a lineage, or, more broadly put, for articulating a symbolic figuration of both synchronic and diachronic patterns of relationship and communication gendered in the feminine, is explicitly declared in the work: one of its protagonists comments, rhetorically addressing a female ancestor, "I am very much aware, Maria Ana . . . , of what you were complaining of, of what you were incapable of: of inventing, all by yourself, the mother, the heroine, the ideology, the myth, the matrix that would give you substance and meaning in the eyes of others, that would open up a path leading to others—if not a path of communication, at least one of shared concerns and anxieties" (212). Another segment of *Novas Cartas* compensates for that remembered instance of solitary impotence (as indeed the book as a whole does) by offering a highly effective dramatization of women's quest for a collective (to paraphrase Virginia Woolf) "meaning of their own." While the scene relies on the familiar formulas of sisterhood and motherhood, the family ties it traces are unmistakably non-literalist, its setting being a convent and the action a dialogue articulated as a responsory chant between, on the one hand, a choir of nuns—"sorores" ("sisters")—and, on the other, their mother abbess, who together collectively catalog exemplary narratives of roles available to women in the traditional society (namely, as nuns, wives, exploited workers, and adulterous lovers). Each exchange is punctuated by the choir of conventual sisters addressing their surrogate mother with a question that has commonly been asked in preparation for revolutions past and future: "What is to be done?" ("And what shall we do, Mother Abbess, what shall we do?" [69]). Thus sisterhood and motherhood are severed from their grounding in the patriarchal model of the family, becoming instead a function of institutional structure and historical experience shared by women, which, even as it oppresses them—as conventual or societal closure—at the same time offers both symbolic and real venues of escape and expansion, manifesting themselves primarily through intellectual and artistic creativity. Soror Mariana is not mentioned in that particular segment of *Novas Cartas*, but her presence and voice remain implicit in the anonymous choir of her sister nuns. As such, she retains her spotlight as an exemplary foremother perhaps even more effectively now that she has lost her solitary prominence and has become reabsorbed into the shared female collectivity.

Another contribution of *Novas Cartas* to the imagining of a female tradition in the national context that does not abound in recorded examples of plausible intellectual foremothers is the authors' invention of the historical lineage of Mariana Alcoforado's female descendants. Mariana herself does not become a biological mother; in fact, the "Three Marias" emphatically deny her that destiny by inventing her pregnancy, but then ending it in a dramatic miscarriage. What we have instead is a succession of *nieces*, daughters of sisters—or perhaps even (and this is an important possibility) daughters of brothers. There is first Soror Mariana's own niece (and namesake), a feminist *avant la lettre* and a politically astute champion of her aunt. Next, several generations later, comes this second Mariana's "direct descendant," a D. Maria Ana, born around 1800, who presents herself as a "spontaneous, philosophically minded offshoot of this female line" (150) whose existence she defines and defends. She demonstrates her independent mind-set by refusing to marry and have children, even as she announces her decision to leave her diary to none other than her niece. Finally, the reader encounters an Ana Maria, born in 1940 (and therefore a contemporary of the authors of *Novas Cartas*) whose plea for "the mother, the heroine, the ideology, the myth, the matrix" I have already quoted above. Thus, by displacing the matrilineal genealogical sequence, the authors free themselves even further from the constraints of the familial metaphor, constraints with which all of its feminist revisions have had to grapple. The fundamental organizing tropes of sisterhood and motherhood are expanded to include female members of an extended family and even male relatives.

In order to further diagnose the effectiveness of deploying the figure of Soror Mariana in the forging of a progressive, feminist "second-order myth," it helps to examine the complex and occasionally conflicted relationship with myth that international feminism has sustained over the last few decades. On the one hand, feminist writers who carried out a critique of representations of women in dominant cultural, social, and political discourses have looked at myth in essentially negative terms, as an arbitrary construct elevated to the status of timeless truth, placed squarely at the service of male-dominated establishment and used to exclude women from its centers of power, political as well as symbolic. Simone de Beauvoir's *The Second Sex* (1949) pioneered this line of inquiry, along with such early North American studies as Betty Friedan's *Feminine Mystique* (1963) or

Mary Ellmann's *Thinking About Women* (1968). On the other hand, an equally abundant body of work has resulted from women's revisionist engagement with myth that has aimed beyond critique and towards reconstruction. From such groundbreaking literary-critical studies as Elaine Showalter's *A Literature of Their Own* (1977) and Sandra Gilbert and Susan Gubar's *Madwoman in the Attic* (1979) to more recent popular blockbusters like Clarissa Pinkola Estés' *Women Who Run With the Wolves*, many writers have practiced mythical "displacement through inversion": "Women take on the mythmaking and, by constructing the other side of well-known plots, displace the narrative focus to insert women into myth" and create demystifying and empowering countermyths (Godard 1991, 6).

Unlike many other historically prominent female figures, whose lives and works, however heavily mythologized over the centuries, are nevertheless a matter of some form of verifiable factual record, Soror Mariana Alcoforado may be considered an almost completely fictional invention, only tenuously supported by historical evidence. Like the Greek poet Sappho, considered by Joan DeJean (1989) as a creature of translation and interpretation, a figment whose features have changed with social mores and aesthetics, Mariana has also been, first and foremost, an eagerly cultivated cultural fiction. *Unlike* Sappho, she most probably never wrote the famous love letters that are her only claim to celebrity and the *raison d'être* of her myth. Which is why it seems expedient to regard her as a mythical sibling of Judith Shakespeare, the nonexistent sister of William famously imagined by Virginia Woolf, even though historical circumstances of their respective processes of invention at a first glance could hardly appear more different. At the same time, as Hilary Owen demonstrates, significant parallels exist between *A Room of One's Own* and the most prominent modern reappropriation of the myth of the Portuguese Nun in *Novas Cartas Portuguesas*. According to Owen, "the Three Marias' *Novas Cartas Portuguesas* and Woolf's *Room* invite comparison on two counts: they use a multiple voice in their treatment of the relationship between gender and writing; and they perform a similar political function in the development of women's writing in their respective national traditions" (1995, 180). To this we might add a comparable proportion of fact and fiction in the stories told in these two books as another aspect that also legitimizes a juxtaposition of Judith Shakespeare and Mariana Alcoforado; however, the primary interest of such a confrontation for the purposes of my argument lies in the gradual transformation of those stories into properly mythical narratives, in other words, narratives validated by a collective stamp of approval as in some sense exemplary and normative. Most crucially, I wish to consider their respective deployment as specifically feminist allegories of historical opportunity and development.

In the decades following the publication of *A Room of One's Own*, but especially since the 1970s, Virginia Woolf's creation has profoundly influenced feminist critics attempting to delineate the tradition of women's writing in English. As Margaret Ezell demonstrates, "links between Woolf's analysis and the contents of current women's literary history are direct and striking. *A Room of One's Own* is cited repeatedly to gloss historical texts and its impact is clearly seen in collections of essays on feminist literary theory. . . . One sees the power of [Woolf's] narrative most clearly in the structure of existing anthologies: almost every anthology which deals with a historical perspective on women's writing cites Woolf's theory of the isolated, self-destructive female artist" (1990, 584–85).[11] Ezell denounces this, to her mind, excessive reliance on the myth of Judith Shakespeare, pointing out that is has served to deny recognition to the many women who did write and even publish in England during the Renaissance and the seventeenth century, according to ample historical evidence unearthed since Woolf's time. Ironically enough, "the initial model of the silenced, alienated Renaissance woman may have been an attempt by a twentieth-century writer to create a voice for her" (583). It appears to have led instead in the opposite direction, reinforcing a mythic stereotype that, by force of changing historical record and circumstance, metamorphosed from a progressive critique of women's oppression into a repressive mechanism of exclusion from a newly minted "tradition" of women's writing.

Judith Shakespeare's example neatly demonstrates both the enduring power of myth and its contradictory nature: by definition, a timeless story of primordial, universal events, it reveals itself in fact to be deeply entangled in history, a narrative whose meaning and function is contingent on "a specific historical moment and discursive practice" (Godard 1991, 9). Elsewhere, we find similar forces at work in the mythical figure of La Malinche, one of the most complex cultural icons of postconquest America, variously imagined as a despicable traitoress to her people, as tragic *La Chingada*, the raped mother of all Mexicans, and finally as a model and inspiration for twentieth-century Mexican and Chicana feminist writers. Particularly for the latter, as Mary Louise Pratt has shown, the "transculturation" of La Malinche into the symbolic repertory of the Chicano movement has provided "a vital, resonant site for defining and symbolizing themselves" and, in particular, "for exploring the often conflicted relations . . . between feminism and ethnic nationalism" (1993, 175).

Not unlike La Malinche, the figure of the Portuguese Nun has acquired a prodigious ability to accommodate a vast repertoire of symbolic and ideological meanings. The authors of *Novas Cartas*, while availing themselves of the mythic potential generated by Soror Mariana's story, demonstrate nevertheless an acute awareness of what Godard calls "the trap of myth": "To vanquish myth from inside is impossible, since every attempt one makes to escape again gets caught up by myth which can only signify the resistance against it" (15). Consequently, they choose to follow the path theorized by Barthes in creating an avowedly artificial myth, which robs mythical speech of its power through intellectual distance and self-reflexive foregrounding of its own ideological intentions. In this, they anticipate deconstructive feminist practice "of continual repetition and oscillation," exploring "the difference of quotation and parody in which the words of the dominant discourse are repeated and re-marked with the difference of deferral" (Godard 1991, 17): Derrida's *différance*.

However, this specifically deconstructive brand of feminist remythification appears to carry with it its own potential discontents. At the heart of feminism are, after all, its political goals: any feminist poetics is validated or discredited by a diagnosis of potential or actual effectiveness of its politics. As some critics of the feminist-deconstructive connection have pointed out, deconstruction's "view from nowhere" and "dream of everywhere" leads to textual practices that "are continually 'slip-sliding' away; through paradox, inversion, self-subversion, facile and intricate textual dance, they often present themselves . . . as having it any way they want. They refuse to assume a shape for which they must take responsibility" (Bordo 1990, 144). While I would argue that the textual politics of *Novas Cartas Portuguesas* are both powerfully feminist and powerfully deconstructive, Susan Bordo's concerns with regard to discursive responsibility appear to be vindicated by a more recent Portuguese literary work, a slim volume of poems by Adília Lopes, who, fifteen years after the publication of *Novas Cartas*, availed herself of the myth of Soror Mariana in a manner quite distinct from Barreno, Horta, and Velho da Costa (although whether that, in turn, entirely discredits it as a feminist gesture remains, in my view, open to debate).

During the period of time separating the two literary incarnations of Mariana Alcoforado, Portuguese culture and society underwent many profound changes and suffered numerous political upheavals to emerge, in the mid-eighties, as a stable Western-style democracy with a steadily growing economy, a solidly centrist government, and a largely depoliti-cized, consumption-oriented popular culture. The radical heyday of the mid-to-late seventies appears, if not forgotten, at least buried in an irre-trievable past; and the place of militant cultural feminism has been taken by something labeled (but rarely if at all examined) as "postfeminism." Lopes, born in the 1960s, is a child of that postrevolutionary, post-every-thing Portugal, and detached and ironic modulations of her poetry contrast markedly with the fervently *engagée* tonality of writing practiced by the authors of *Novas Cartas*. Her volume, entitled *Marquês de Chamilly: Kabale und Liebe*, contains some lovely modernizing glosses of the seventeenth-century passion: Mariana travels by subway, ponders the mysteries of postal zip codes, and scribbles "M.A. loves Ch." (in English in the original) on steamed-up windowpanes. However, the theme that gains increasing prominence as the sequence develops is that of ever-escalating deferral and displacement of Mariana's amorous discourse: her letters are lost or misdirected by the post, dropped by a careless mailman in a Parisian street. Finally, Chamilly does write back, but only to explain politely that he had never been able to decipher his insistent correspon-dent's handwriting and to request, would she perhaps print her next missive in block capitals? The last poem takes this epistolary affair "slip-slidin'" away into a potentially endless *mise en abîme* of simulacra, as it brings in another nun and another marquis, who also happen to be named Mariana Alcoforado and Chamilly, but whose distracted correspondence bears no resemblance whatsoever to the "original" Portuguese Nun's passionate discourse. As a final gesture, the other nun and her other mar-quis shrug their respective shoulders in weary unison: Mariana's love, to say nothing of her weighty mythical roles, including that of a recovered foremother to the feminist movement of the seventies and beyond, is swallowed by a whirlpool of textual fragmentation, displacement, and misinterpretation. A cynical anti-myth for a jaded *fim-do-século*, Lopes's "Mariana" no longer stands for anything, and, unlike most of her earlier incarnations, she appears to carry no ideological banners at all. Which per-haps serves to demonstrate that myth, besides being infinitely susceptible to historical change, is also not immune to entropy.

Epilogue: The Mértola Window

Throughout the long history of textual interpretation and cultural invention that has followed in the wake of the original publication of the *Lettres portugaises*, one recurrent image in particular has registered an enduring and arresting presence. It has remained centrally poised within the repository of both *alcoforadista* and anti-*alcoforadista* discourse, specifically owing to its contentious deployment within the authorship controversy, but also as a result of its independently strong visual and dramatic appeal. That image is the famous *janela de Mértola* (or, as the French text has it, "le balcon d'où l'on voit Mertola"), the window, balcony, or gallery from which the epistolary Mariana catches her first glimpse of the dashing French lieutenant, and which continues to play a significant role in the scenario of her love story. The prominence given to the ambiguous parapet in interpretive accounts arguing for or against the authenticity of the nun's letters has been due primarily to the lack of congruence between the French original of the *Lettres portugaises* and the material reality of the Portuguese setting it glosses: one cannot see Mértola from any "balcon" or window in Beja, since that relatively nearby town is separated from the capital of Lower Alentejo by some elevated terrain. It should be recognized that the *alcoforadista* tradition has dealt imaginatively and even convincingly with this referential obstacle. Briefly, "Mértola" of the French text is taken to refer not to the town itself, but rather to the road leading out of Beja in its direction and to the gate in the old city walls through which the road passed and which, for that reason, was known as "Portas de Mértola," the Mértola Gate. The Mértola Gate could effectively be seen from the nearby Convento da Conceição. According to this interpretation, the French translator of the nun's letters betrayed his lack of familiarity with their local setting by carelessly distorting the topographic reference, which the lost Portuguese original was certain to express in its proper form.[1]

However, the most intriguing aspect of the reference to the "Mértola Window" does not reside in its factual relevance in the context of authorial validation of the *Lettres portugaises,* but rather in a larger, metaphorical potential carried by this central image. As Graça Abreu comments, the impossible "Mértola" of the French text gains in suggestive richness of signification what it appears to lose in verisimilitude, becoming in fact

The Mértola Window in the Convento da Conceição in Beja. Photograph by António Cunha.

a central trope for the polymorphous elusiveness of the entire *Lettres por-tugaises*: "Mértola could be the image of all the answers that the text does not give us, even as it pretends to show us ways to obtain them" (87). Along with many other aspects of the Portuguese Nun's story, but perhaps more clearly so than any other, the *janela de Mértola* may thus be de-scribed as a figure pointing toward and actively stimulating the twin movements of displacement and deferral that have historically informed interpretation of the *Lettres portugaises*. It functions in this way even in the relatively restricted context of the authorship dispute. A territorially specific point of reference, it is first revealed as such in the French text, where its exotic and yet exact presence serves as a seal of factual authen-ticity, legitimizing the letters' foreignness. It appears to lose its territorial authority upon being regrafted back onto its presumably native ground, where it does not match local reality, and as a result it is taken to signify instead the text's fictitious mendacity. However, just a slight refiguring of "Mértola"'s referential meaning suffices to not only restore but in fact re-inforce the letters' veracity, while relegating the stigma of ignorance and betrayal to their French *traduttore tradittore*. As an icon transported across time, space, and ideological agendas, the Mértola Window never ceases to signify nor to inspire a continuing proliferation of meanings; and it comes as no surprise that the image should carry its fertile potential over into fields of discourse and cultural production which are increas-ingly remote—in geographic as well as substantive terms—both from its original setting in a seventeenth-century literary classic of amorous lament and from its modern revival as a central element in a prominent "invented tradition" of modern Portuguese nationality. In these final pages, the figure of *janela de Mértola* will therefore provide a point of departure from my predominantly allegorical and geopolitically situated reading of the myth of Mariana Alcoforado, where I have stressed the story's cultural and anthropological significance as one of particularly in-teresting (because of its ambiguous and convoluted nature) master fictions shaping the self-knowledge of nineteenth- and twentieth-century Por-tuguese society. Opening up this interpretive scenario instead of providing it with a conclusive closure is meant to help invite further exploration of other paths, apertures, and lookouts (not only those pointing towards Mér-tola) discernible in the labyrinthine history of this slight yet almost im-probably consequential text.

Arguably the most complex and influential contemporary recasting of the dilemma of the *Lettres portugaises* may be found in a debate between two prominent feminist critics, Nancy K. Miller and Peggy Kamuf, which centered on the issue of the theoretical and ideological significance of the text's authorship and its relationship to the politics of feminist scholarship as practiced in the United States in the context of the then-emergent academic discipline of women's studies. In what would turn out to be the debate's first installment, provided by Kamuf's article "Writing Like a Woman" (1980), the writer argued against "the tautological assumption that a feminine 'identity' is one which signs itself with a feminine name," and proposed instead an analytic direction that would take as its point of departure "looking behind the mask of the proper name"; as her test case Kamuf chose the *Lettres portugaises*, a text that "in the absence of a signature, must be read blind, as if no known subject had written it" (286). During a Symposium on Feminist Criticism held at Cornell University in October 1981, Kamuf restated her conviction with regard to what she described as "one of the primary limitations of an assumption guiding much current feminist scholarship: an unshaken faith in the ultimate arrival at essential truth through the empirical method of accumulation of knowledge, knowledge about women" (1990, 109). In the course of the symposium, Kamuf's deconstructive critique was challenged by Miller's forceful defense of the need to "continue to work for the woman who has been writing," an argument based as well on textual and ideological implications carried by indeterminate authorship of the *Lettres portugaises*:

> What bothers me about the metalogically "correct" position is what I take to be its necessary implications for practice: that by glossing "woman" as an archaic signifier, it glosses over the *referential* suffering of women. . . . More locally, it doesn't matter to Kamuf's reading whether the *Portuguese Letters* were written by a woman or by a man, but it does to mine. (1990, 114–15; original emphasis)

The Kamuf/Miller debate (which extended through subsequent publication of the two interventions in an issue of the journal *Diacritics* called "*Cherchez la femme*: Feminist Critique/Feminine Text," and which attracted much further commentary) was given a sort of a closure when it was reprinted in the volume *Conflicts in Feminism,* edited by Marianne Hirsch and Evelyn Fox Keller. There, Kamuf's "Replacing Feminist Criticism" and Miller's "The Text's Heroine: A Feminist Critic and Her Fictions" are followed by the two critics' collectively written "Parisian Letters" (subtitled "Between Feminism and Deconstruction"). Miller begins this epistolary exchange by identifying the scene of her writing, the terrace of a stone house in Provence:

I've known since I came here for the month of July that I wanted to begin our correspondence—physically—from this place: from the terrace. Writing from the terrace is a trope I associate with you, or rather by association, with the scene of writing in which . . . you imagined the Portuguese nun: a problematic female subject, writing from the balcony, from her abandonment. (1990, 121)

In this fashion, Mariana's *janela de Mértola* becomes recast as the stone terrace of a Provençal vacation house and, simultaneously, as a metaphorical point of both contact and difference within a dialogue between two feminist scholars working along the Franco-American connection, who write, against the grain of tradition, "not as *confidantes*, the canonical female letter writer, but as the academic equivalent of *femmes de lettres* about a theoretical conflict between us" (121). In the manner already explored by the authors of *Novas Cartas Portuguesas*, Miller and Kamuf's epistolary exchange absorbs and reframes Mariana's anguished soliloquy in a textual environment informed by shared feminist concerns and female solidarity. At the same time, however, their concluding statement emerges as one of the most radically deterritorializing acts of referential displacement in the critical history of the seventeenth-century text. It rewrites the *Lettres portugaises* as "Parisian Letters" (which here in fact circulate between Paris and the south of France) from a perspective informed by ideological and institutional concerns of academic feminism in the United States, while preserving referentially precise metaphorical trappings of the "scene of writing" represented by the original five epistles. By doing so, this conclusion of the Kamuf/Miller exchange does not merely remove the text's interpretation from its traditional moorings in either the monologic context of the French literary canon or the bilateral Franco-Portuguese (mis)communication. It performs a properly globalizing gesture, which preserves static locality (the Mértola window *qua* the Provençal terrace) as an apparently indispensable element of affective referentiality, but which gains its signifying impetus precisely owing to the movement of borderless, free-floating displacement that it generates.

A very distinct, and yet in some ways comparable, example of such a displacement may be found in what is, to my knowledge, the only film ever made that has availed itself explicitly of the theme of the Portuguese Nun.[2] It happens to be a pornographic movie appealing to S&M-oriented viewers, directed by Jess (Jesús) Franco in 1977 and described by *An A-Z Guide to Erotic Horror Films on Videocassette* as "a near-masterpiece . . . easily one of [Franco's] most satisfying and spectacular pictures to date."

Entitled *Love Letters of a Portuguese Nun*, this German-Swiss coproduction appears to be shot entirely on location in Portugal and it features a few Portuguese actors, albeit in minor roles, among its broadly international cast. I was unable to determine what language (if any) the actors shared in the film's original version, since the dialogue on the tape I rented from a video store in Athens, Georgia, was entirely dubbed in English, although the subtitles were in what I finally managed to identify as Finnish. It should not, perhaps, come as a complete surprise that the story told by the picture has nothing whatsoever to do with the love affair of Mariana Alcoforado and Chevalier de Chamilly, being instead an account of a young woman's forced induction into a convent and of sexual horrors she suffers there at the hands of her superiors. It is somewhat more puzzling, given the film's title, that no love letters at all are written or referred to in the course of its events: the only epistle featured there is a plea for help addressed to God by the protagonist (named "Marie" and sometimes referred to as "Maria" or "Maria Rosalia"). In her letter, Marie complains about being subjected to gory Satanic rituals and much sadistic abuse, which are minutely depicted throughout the movie, at one point involving eager participation by Satan himself (an early Bela Lugosi look-alike who goes about dressed in a cheesy red jumpsuit). In spite of the letter-writing scene's remoteness from its source in the *Lettres portugaises*, it does in fact feature a window and a passing horseman: he is the improbably named "Prince Manuel Gonzales of Portugal" who picks up the letter Marie manages to drop from her cell and who eventually becomes the nun's savior.

The convent, named "Serradayres" and described by one character as "the most beautiful abbey in Portugal," is one of two architecturally prominent buildings appearing in the picture; the other one plays the role of "the Grand Inquisitor's palace," but it can be unmistakably identified by any viewer acquainted with Portugal as Lisbon's monumental Mosteiro dos Jerónimos. It is in the beautiful basilica of the Mosteiro, with its stained-glass windows and tombs of Camões and Vasco da Gama, that the film's final scene, the seizing of Satanic perverts by royal authorities, takes place. Mind-boggling as it is to realize that the picture's producers must have managed to obtain official permission to shoot their concluding scenes in one of Portugal's most solemn public spaces (London's Westminster Abbey or Notre Dame of Paris come to mind as equivalents), the vibrant yet chaotic atmosphere of the Portuguese mid-1970s, following the Revolution of 25 de Abril, may help explain the filmmakers' success in obtaining their license. More important, the incongruous juxtaposition of, on the one hand, the cosmopolitan, linguistically unstable, and historically flippant aesthetic code of Franco's *Love Letters of a Portuguese Nun* and, on the other, the prominently authentic if misrepresented visual reference of the Mosteiro once again activates what we might call the "Mértola Window effect," in which territorial signifiers play dizzying hide-and-seek with their readers' or viewers' perceptions. Furthermore, the thoroughly internationalized circuit of production and distribution characteristic of the porn movie industry helps produce another instance of radical deterritorialization of the original *Lettres portugaises*. A Spanish-language poster of the film arbitrarily changes its title, which becomes *Love Letters to a Nun*, with the word *Portuguese* ("portuguesa") tucked underneath in much smaller type (an interesting cultural comment in its own right), even as it pretends to acknowledge the literary reference it appropriates: the letters are said to have been "prohibited and censored for three centuries" and now "filmed for the first time."[3]

A different sort of international dissemination is represented by two recent reprises of Mariana Alcoforado's story in the linguistic and cultural sphere of *Lusofonia*, the Portuguese-speaking world. In Portugal itself, as I have already suggested, after the spectacular exploration of its symbolic and ideological potential in *Novas Cartas Portuguesas*, the myth appears to have reached its point of exhaustion (even as it remains firmly entrenched in the pop-cultural repository of nationally representative fictions) and its truth value is no longer viewed as an issue worth considering, much less supporting. By contrast, the two texts I am about to discuss invest strongly and unambiguously in the seemingly anachronistic notions of Mariana's Portuguese authenticity and historical veracity of her authorship of the *Lettres portugaises*. One of them is the novel *Mariana* (1997) by the Californian writer Katherine Vaz, whose publishing debut *Saudade* (1994) received some critical acclaim as the first novel in the U.S. about Portuguese-Americans. Unlike the "Three Marias" twenty-five years earlier, Vaz does not take the radical path of formal experiment and freewheeling remythification of the book's pre-text; her fictional reconstruction (charmingly dedicated to "a Frenchman who stayed") is concerned with the real, historical Mariana, and Vaz faithfully follows the *alcoforadista* gospel in bringing back to life the story of the prodigious nun's love, abandonment, and subsequent literary accomplishment. Vaz's passionately serious approach to reclaiming the *Lettres portugaises* for Mariana and her homeland, which the writer emphasizes in her afterword, also manifests itself throughout her work: standard arguments on behalf of the nun's authorship are woven into the narrative fabric of the novel in ways that are sometimes ingenious, but occasionally result in stilted passages whose only function appears to be providing support for the plausibility of Portuguese provenance of the text. On the other hand, Vaz's local references are impeccably researched and carefully explained in an appended glossary, which includes the inevitable Mértola with its corresponding lookout (1997, 318):

> **Mértola**: A small town in Southern Portugal, near the Guadiana River. There was a now-famous "Mértola Window" at the Convent of Conceição in Beja, so-called not because one could see this town from the window or balcony, but because it looked out on the southern gates and road that led the 54 kilometers to Mértola. It was from this window that we are certain that Mariana first saw the Count of Chamilly.

Although Vaz's novel has by now been translated into Portuguese and published in Portugal (by Edições ASA), it does not seem to have generated much publicity in Mariana's homeland, certainly nothing even remotely comparable to the outpouring of commentary that followed the publication of Luciano Cordeiro's *Soror Mariana* in 1888 or the political impact of *Novas Cartas Portuguesas* in the 1970s. This lukewarm response may be due as much to the exhaustion of the myth's power to inflame popular imagination as to the fact that Vaz refuses to "make new" on the basis of her meticulously gathered material: in spite, or perhaps precisely because, of her diasporic perspective, the writer chooses to reproduce the myth and the reality of its territorial setting in the most orthodox and faithful manner imaginable. Paradoxically, it is her knowledgeable respect for the *alcoforadista* tradition that may have robbed her work of a potential to influence the culture she so lovingly and compellingly describes.

The principle of rigorous fidelity may be said to have become both affirmed and subverted in another "Lusophone" reclaiming of the *Lettres portugaises*, namely in what is, to my knowledge, the latest translation (or "retroversion," as its author prefers to call it) of the French text into Portuguese. Published in 1992 by the Brazilian Imago Editora, these *Cartas de Amor* were translated by Marilene Felinto, an author best known for her 1982 novel *As Mulheres de Tijucopapo [The Women of Tijucopapo]* and who, upon the book's translation into English, "has been hailed in the United States as an important new black woman writer giving voice to the experiences of the marginal in society" (Matthews 1994, 131). Felinto's reprise of the *Lettres portugaises*, similarly to Vaz's novel, remains firmly rooted in the canonical *alcoforadista* perspective: Mariana Alcoforado appears as the author of the letters both on the book's cover and in the cataloging data printed inside, where the name of Guilleragues is never mentioned. Felinto herself proves to be a staunch (if somewhat erratically informed) partisan of the nun's authorship, claiming in her preface that any doubts which might still be evoked in this respect had been eliminated by "various Portuguese and French scholarly studies" (Alcoforado 1992, 13). Felinto's postcolonial Lusophone perspective does, however, manifest itself in her version of the French text: her *Cartas de Amor* follow relaxed colloquial cadences of contemporary Brazilian Portuguese in what is likely to be one of the most "domesticating" translations of the *Lettres portugaises* into any language or linguistic variant. In terms suggested by Friedrich Schleiermacher's seminal essay, "On the Different Methods of Translating" (1813), to follow a "domesticating method" equals, according to Lawrence Venuti, "an ethnocentric reduction of the foreign text to target-language cultural values," an attitude which should be resisted and denounced as a colonial and imperial legacy, to be replaced by a "foreignizing" approach, "an ethnodeviant pressure on those values to register the linguistic and cultural difference of the foreign text" (1995, 20). Felinto's translation of the *Lettres portugaises* disturbs, however, ideological neatness of this strategic binary on several levels: a postcolonial rendition of a text that, for all its metropolitan canonicity, remains in many respects radically and irreducibly "minor," it domesticates its object's foreignness by adapting it to a cultural idiom that, in spite of its extra-European marginality, may be considered in fact, because of the sheer number of its speakers and of its global dissemination through visual mass media, *the* dominant version of Portuguese spoken in the world today. Here is Felinto's seductive rendering of the famous initial sentence of the *Lettres portugaises* ("Considère, mon amour, jusqu'à quel excès tu as manqué de prévoyance"): "Pense no quanto você não conseguiu prever o que aconteceria, meu amor" (Alcoforado 1992, 17). Removed from its context, it could easily be perceived as a line taken from a scene in one of Brazil's fabulously popular and widely exported *telenovelas*, or soap operas. The Brazilian translator's stylistic option results thus in an unpredictable dislocation both of the original text and of its earlier Portuguese versions into a new, distinct sphere of cultural production and consumption where its basic plot line of love, abandonment, and betrayal is reconfigured in terms suggestive of contemporary mass media melodramas.

Curiously enough, a crucial passage of Mariana's "Second Letter," which contains the notorious and treacherous reference to Mértola, is translated by Felinto with no concern for its significance within the authorship debate: *le balcon d'où l'on voit Mertola* becomes simply and faithfully *a varanda de onde se avista Mértola* (28). Mértola is thus returned to its original status as an impossible territorial signifier, in spite of its translator's emphatically affirmed belief in the Portuguese authenticity of the text, and this internal contradiction of Felinto's version (however unintentional it appears to be) effectively mirrors the referential elusiveness of the *Lettres portugaises* and becomes a fitting addition to the rich repository of ironies, paradoxes, and dissonances found in the history of its interpretations.

Notes

PROLOGUE: WHAT REALLY HAPPENED

1. The Cologne edition, by Pierre du Marteau, was titled *Lettres d'amour d'une religieuse escrites au chevalier de C. officier françois en Portugal* and contained the following notice: "The name of the person to whom they were written is Monsieur le Chevalier de Chamilly; and the name of the person who translated them is Cuilleraque" [Le nom de celui auquel on les a écrites, est Monsieur le Chevalier de Chamilly; et le nom de celui qui en a fait la traduction est Cuilleraque (Guilleragues 1962, viii)]. The Amsterdam edition, by Isaac Van Dick, bore the title *Lettres d'une religieuse portugaise traduites en françois*. For a recent comprehensive listing of preserved editions of the French text published in the seventeenth, eighteenth, and nineteenth centuries, see Alcover 1985, 644–48.

2. In addition to François Jost's seminal study of the genre, see also Susan Lee Carrel, *Le Soliloque de la passion féminine ou le dialogue illusoire: étude d'une formule monophonique de la littérature épistolaire* (Tübingen: Gunter Narr Verlag, and Paris: Éditions Jean-Michel Place, 1982). Carrel adopts Jost's designation of "le type portugais" in her study of the monophonic variety of epistolary discourse (letters addressed by a woman to her lover and presented without the lover's responses), thus highlighting the importance of *Lettres portugaises* as the modern prototype of this genre. For an insightful summary and critique of Carrel's book, see Janet Altman, "Portuguese Writing and Women's Consciousness: The Loneliness of the Long Distance Lover," *Degré Second: Studies in French Literature* 7 (July 1983): 163–75.

3. Boissonade's revelation was based on a handwritten note of unknown origin, which he had come upon in his copy of the *Lettres portugaises*. According to his testimony, the note read as follows: "The nun who wrote these letters was named Mariana Alcaforada. She was a nun living in Beja, between Estremadura and Andalusia. The gentleman to whom these letters were written was the Count of Chamilly, also called the Count of Saint-Léger." [La religieuse qui a écrit ces lettres se nommoit Mariane Alcaforada, religieuse à Beja, entre l'Estramadure et l'Andalousie. Le cavalier à qui ces lettres furent écrites étoit le comte de Chamilly, dit alors le comte de Saint-Léger (quoted in Rodrigues 1935, 91)].

4. For a more detailed account of the early history of reception and interpretation of the *Lettres portugaises* in France see Frédéric Deloffre and Jacques Rougeot, "L'Histoire des *Lettres portugaises*" in Guilleragues 1972, 61–93. Deloffre and Rougeot divide the

critical fortune of the letters into three distinct periods: "impressionistic," through the end of the eighteenth century (including the *Notice* of Mercier de Saint-Léger); "historical," dominated by fact-finding labors of nineteenth-century Portuguese researchers; and the modern "critical" period, inaugurated in 1926 by F. C. Green, and culminating with Deloffre and Rougeot's own, self-described "definitive" edition, which attributed the authorship of the text to Gabriel-Joseph de Lavergne de Guilleragues.

5. See, however, Wolfgang Leiner's review of Yves Florenne's edition of *Lettres de la Religieuse portugaise* in the collection *Le livre de poche classique* (Paris: Librairie Générale Française, 1979), in which Leiner, a leading scholar of French seventeenth-century literature, states that Florenne's arguments in favor of the letters' authenticity "force us to reopen the file that we probably closed too quickly" (1980, 146). For a stalwart *guilleraguiste* reply to these and other challenges, consult Frédéric Deloffre's successive updates: "Le bilan du quart de siècle: les *Lettres portugaises* et la critique" in *Quaderni di filologia e lingue romanze*, 1984: 119–67; and "Les *Lettres portugaises*" in *L'Information litteraire* 41, 5 (Nov.–Dec. 1989): 7–12. Regarding the literary strategy of *dépaysement*, it became such a commonly employed device that one eighteenth-century French publisher of a work titled *Lettres saxones* was to comment on an astounding proliferation of epistolary fictions arriving "des pays les plus barbares" (Larat 1928, 625).

6. Spitzer's essay was first published in French in *Romanische Forschungen* 65 (1954): 94–135, and reprinted in his collection of essays *Romanische Literaturstudien, 1936–56* (Tübingen: Niemeyer, 1959). I have quoted from the English translation by David Bellos. For feminist critiques of Spitzer's argument, see Peggy Kamuf, "Writing Like a Woman," in *Women and Language in Literature and Society*, ed. Sally McConnell-Ginet, Ruth Borker, and Nelly Furman (New York: Praeger, 1980), 284–99, and Linda S. Kauffman, *Discourses of Desire* (Ithaca: Cornell University Press, 1986), 97–98.

7. Although the place of the *Lettres portugaises* in French literary tradition and the text's deployment in theoretical negotiations referentially rooted in the Western European canon are only tangentially germane to the objectives of this study, some additional highlights of critical literature merit reference here. In addition to the sources already cited, see also Wolfgang Leiner's introduction to the issue of *Papers on French Seventeenth-Century Literature* dedicated to the *Lettres portugaises* (*Actes de New Orleans*, 1982): 17–102. For a comprehensive, stimulating reexamination of the text's interpretive tradition, consult Claire Goldstein's article, "Love Letters: Discourses of Gender and Writing in the Criticism of the *Lettres portugaises*" (*The Romanic Review* 88, 4 [1997]: 571–90). Perhaps the most enduringly eloquent testimony to the continuing appeal and relevance of the *Lettres portugaises* in the context of contemporary theoretical and ideological debates within literary studies in the United States may be found in the exchange between Peggy Kamuf and Nancy K. Miller regarding the issue of female authorship and the politics of feminist scholarship (see the Epilogue for a more comprehensive account of this critical dialogue).

CHAPTER I. LOVE AND PARANOIA ON A CULTURAL PERIPHERY

1. Prior to its inclusion in his *Pela mão de Alice. O social e o político na pós-modernidade.* (Porto: Afrontamento, 1994), Sousa Santos's essay had been published and

reprinted in the journals *Via Latina* (1991, 58–64), *Novos Estudos CEBRAP* (34 [1992]: 136–55), and *Luso-Brazilian Review* (29 [1992]: 97–113).

2. Unless otherwise indicated, all translations from the Portuguese are my own.

3. The study of historical "invention of tradition" and "national memory" has in recent years been the subject of several individual and collective Portuguese publications, such as, in a chronological order, Sérgio Campos Matos, *História, Mitologia, Imaginário Nacional. A História no Curso dos Liceus (1895–1939)* (Lisboa: Horizonte, 1990); Francisco Bethencourt and Diogo Ramada Curto, eds., *A Memória da Nação* (Lisboa: Sá da Costa, 1991); Yvette Kace Centeno, ed., *Portugal: Mitos Revisitados* (Lisboa: Salamandra, 1993); *O Imaginário do Império*, special issue of the historical journal *Penélope* 15 (1995), among others.

4. A term of certain currency in Portuguese and European cultural discourse, "imagology" is described by one practitioner as "a field of study of comparatist and Franco-German origin which concentrates on textual analysis of ethnic images in literature"; what "lies at the heart of imagology" is the "idea that national identity is an image rather than essential structure" (Spiering, 10).

5. It could be argued, of course, that such protean plasticity is the very condition of survival and continuing appeal of all enduring cultural symbols. See AbdoolKarim A. Vakil's (1996) fascinating discussion of changing representations of the Portuguese "Discoveries" and their inscription in the rhetoric of national identity.

6. For an abundantly annotated overview of contemporary Portuguese writings on national identity see Almeida 1991 and 1994.

7. The use of the terms "core" and "periphery" to describe worldwide patterns of development dates back to the activities of the U.N. Economic Commission on Latin America in the late 1940s and early 1950s (Wallerstein 1982, 91).

8. A comprehensive presentation of the development and current state of world-system studies is obviously beyond the scope of this chapter. For a programmatic introduction, see Terence K. Hopkins, Immanuel Wallerstein, et al., *World-Systems Analysis: Theory and Methodology* (Beverly Hills, London, and New Delhi: Sage Publications, 1982).

9. One recent important contribution is the volume of essays edited by Anthony D. King, *Culture, Globalization and the World-System* (Minneapolis: University of Minnesota Press, 1997). For an earlier example of interdisciplinary application of a global perspective in political economy, see Kasja Ekholm and Jonathan Friedman, "Towards a Global Anthropology," in *History and Underdevelopment. Essays on Underdevelopment and European Expansion in Asia and Africa*, ed. L. Blussé, H. L. Wesseling, and G. D. Winius (Leiden: Leiden University, 1980), 61–76.

10. See also, for example, the issue of *Canadian Review of Comparative Literature* on the special topic of "Postcolonial Literatures: Theory and Practice" (22, 3–4 [Sept.-Dec. 1995]). Following sections devoted to Middle Eastern, East Indian, African, North American, Latin American, and Caribbean "postcolonialities," a substantial segment of the issue is occupied by reports on contemporary developments in the literatures of East Central Europe. Steven Tötösy, as one of the issue's editors, provides the following justification in his introductory essay:

> Based on the assumption that the former USSR may be understood as centre by its political, military, economic, and ideological parameters in its relationship with its satellite countries, East Central European literatures are understood as the periphery in relation to the Soviet centre and consequently, as post-colonial situations. (400–41)

11. In fact, as Onésimo T. Almeida points out, very few Portuguese authors have addressed the issue of Spanish-Portuguese identity, "because a direct confrontation of both countries' common identities is almost a national taboo in Portugal" (1994, 157). Almeida cites nevertheless the late Natália Correia, the most prominent writer among the minority of Portuguese *iberistas*, and her book *Somos Todos Hispanos* (Lisboa: O Jornal, 1988) with its "interesting defence of the commonalities among Hispanic cultures" (Almeida, 162).

12. For a discussion of the concept of national allegory and its applicability to the case of the Portuguese Nun, see chapter 2: Inventing Mariana.

13. As reported in the daily *Diário do Alentejo* (vol. 1, no. 3325). Incidentally, it was at the Beja Círculo that Simone de Beauvoir made her first public appearance in Portugal, during her 1945 tour, with a lecture on "La Vie et les lettres en France de l'occupation à la liberation." It is not known what, if anything, she may have had to say on that occasion about the Portuguese Nun. In her novel *The Mandarins* (1954; English translation 1956), which relies in part on Beauvoir's impressions from her tour, Beja barely flickers past the protagonist's car windows (as indeed does much of Portugal). However, its streets are said to have echoed "the ancient cries of a lovesick nun" (100).

14. Alberto Telles's *Lord Byron em Portugal* (Lisboa: Diário de Portugal, 1879) is a book-long reappraisal of the case, whose title page carries an epigraph from *Macbeth*: "Such welcome and unwelcome things at once, / 'Tis hard to reconcile." An even more extensive commentary may be found in D. G. Dalgado's *Lord Byron's Childe Harold's Pilgrimage to Portugal, Critically Examined* (Lisboa: Imprensa Nacional, 1919). For more recent critical accounts, see João Gaspar Simões, "Lorde Byron, o seu poema *Childe Harold* e o que nele se diz de Portugal," in *O Primeiro de Janeiro*, 11 de Janeiro 1976 (caderno); J. Almeida Flor, "Uma recensão portuguesa de *Childe Harold's Pilgrimage*," in *Byron Portugal 1977* (Lisbon: Portuguese Committee of the Byron Society and Instituto de Cultura Portuguesa, 1977), 137–51; and F. de Mello Moser, "Byron and Portugal: The Progress of an Offending Pilgrim," in *Byron's Political and Cultural Influence in Nineteenth-Century Europe: A Symposium*, ed. Paul Graham Trueblood (Atlantic Highlands, N.J.: Humanities Press, 1981), 132–42.

Chapter 2. Inventing Mariana

1. "Women know neither how to describe nor experience love itself. . . . I would bet everything I have that the *Portuguese Letters* were written by a man" (transl. by Peggy Kamuf; quoted in Kauffman 1986, 94–95). Interestingly, however, Camilo's denial of Portuguese female authorship was not predicated on stereotyped notions of gendered identity, but rather on a lack of stylistic affinity between Mariana's letters and literary works produced by such seventeenth-century Portuguese women writers as Bernarda de Lacerda and Violante da Cruz (107).

2. I am adhering to standard Portuguese usage by referring to Camilo Castelo Branco as "Camilo" rather than as "Castelo Branco." Similarly, in future citations Teófilo Braga's name will be reiterated as "Teófilo" rather than as "Braga."

3. As Rui Ramos notes, "There is not a single important politician in the second half of the nineteenth century who does not have his name and list of publications featured in Inocêncio Francisco da Silva's bibliographic dictionary" (1994, 44).

4. According to Rui Ramos, the Geographical Society of Lisbon, founded on 11 November 1879, was where "African enthusiasts engaged in convincing affluent individuals that the colonies were the great market of the future" (1994, 30). Along with the Society for Commercial Geography based in Porto, it acted as the most powerful instrument of colonial propaganda, promoting the establishment of a Portuguese empire in Africa that would reach "from sea coast to sea coast" (31–32).

5. Regrettably, Jameson does not expound further on this notion, returning to the binary framework of his argument and failing to address what to my mind is a necessary question: What is the historical, cultural and geopolitical location of the reading subject who thus freely chooses whether to interpret semiperipheral narratives as either primarily "social" or primarily "individual" and according to what criterion is the choice being made?

6. Oliveira Martins responded with a letter of such extravagant praise that the publishers chose to quote it in their introduction to the second edition of *Soror Mariana*: "You have performed a miracle. Your book on the *Cartas* is truly definitive; there is nothing left to say. You have exhausted all erudition and criticism: there is no point in investigating or elaborating any further" (Cordeiro 1891, 9).

7. It is important to remark at this point that the British-Portuguese conflict over the two countries' colonial territories in East Africa, with the Ultimatum as its climactic central event, figures as an extremely minor incident in general histories of the Scramble for Africa, meriting no mention at all—to give but one example—in Thomas Pakenham's recent voluminous account, *The Scramble for Africa, 1876–1912* (New York: Random House, 1991).

8. Conde de Ficalho, "A Freira portuguesa" (originally published in Lisbon's *Repórter*; reprinted in *Jornal da noite*, 28 August 1888).

9. In the years 1936 to 1945, at least fourteen articles, reviews, and notes dedicated to Soror Mariana were published in *Diário do Alentejo*.

10. "A nun here allegedly had a steamy affair with a French officer and wrote her story in *Letters of a Portuguese Nun* in 1669. Soon after publication, the letters were translated into French and became an immediate literary success. Questions have surfaced as to the real author of the poetry, but it still makes a nice story," in *Let's Go! The Budget Guide to Spain, Portugal and Morocco* (New York: St. Martin's Press, 1989), 427.

11. "At the end of the gallery there is a grated window, better known as the 'window of Mariana' repeatedly mentioned in the famous *Cartas de Amor* by Mother Mariana Alcoforado, a nun in the Convento da Conceição." The museum's visitors' book registers, in fact, some complaints with regard to this lack of emphasis and scarcity of information on the convent's historically most famous inhabitant.

12. As Saramago wrote, his considerations of the figure of Soror Mariana appear "outside of the context of this historical essay" (9), a remark whose import did not outweigh, however, marketing considerations that appear to have led to the choice of the book's title.

13. The author was Pedro Víctor Sequeira (signed "P. V."), one of the many reviewers of Luciano Cordeiro's *Soror Mariana*, whose article was originally published in *Correio da Manhã* and reprinted in Cordeiro's *Jornal da Noite* (17 September 1888). Sequeira seems to have pioneered the tradition of picturing the last of the Alcoforados as a miserable degenerate and thus reenforcing the organic metaphor of flourishing and decay that typically structures genealogical narratives, including that of Mariana's family.

CHAPTER 3. TRANSLATING MARIANA

1. I have registered the following translators of the *Lettres portugaises* into Portuguese, many of whose "versions" have gone into multiple editions (dates in the parentheses refer to their original publication): Filinto Elísio (1819), José Maria de Sousa Botelho (1924), Lopes de Mendonça (1852), Domingos José Enes (1872), Luciano Cordeiro (1888), Joaquim Gomes (1902), Manuel Ribeiro (1913), Jaime Cortesão (1920), Afonso Lopes Vieira (1941), Eugénio de Andrade (1969), Marilene Felinto (1992).

2. The often repeated assertion of Chamilly's despicable doltishness can be traced back to an opinion that the memorialist Saint-Simon had voiced in his comment on the occasion of the Marshal of France's death in 1715: "He was a big, tall man, well built, and of great merit . . . but his lack of wit always surprised people and very much embarrassed his wife, who was quite sharp herself" (quoted in Guilleragues 1972, 72).

3. This is not to say that Fonseca's militant and rambunctious (as well as anachronistic) intervention had genuine scholarly merit comparable to that of Deloffre and Rougeot's equally militant, but incomparably better fundamented and more convincing study, but merely to point out that its author was affected, from the very beginning, by a sense of laboring against, so to speak, geoculturally overwhelming odds.

4. I am quoting from the English translation of a collection of Freyre's essays published in Lisbon in 1961 to mark the commemorations of the five-hundredth anniversary of the death of Prince Henry the Navigator. Both the Portuguese original and the English translation carry the imprimatur of the official state Executive Committee for the celebrations.

5. At the risk of pointing out the obvious, it is nevertheless necessary to mention that the polar opposition between the Golden Age of the Portuguese history in the fifteenth and sixteenth centuries and the country's state of decadence in later times was largely a retrospective mythical construct. As Rui Ramos comments, "Imperial exploits of the sixteenth and seventeenth centuries had disguised [Portugal's] natural poverty, putting into circulation the notion that the country, as the Republican writer José Felix Henriques Nogueira wrote in 1851, had once been 'rich, great and powerful' and only in the present did it appear as 'poor, small and ridiculed'" (1994, 23). Such tendency is of course not unique to Portugal, as Peter Boerner makes clear in pointing to an inclination, common in modern nationalism, to "interpret periods of high cultural achievement as acmes of national identity" (1986, 15).

6. The late eighteenth- and nineteenth-century vogue of Camões as an *avant la lettre* incarnation of a Romantic *poète maudit* was not limited to Portugal. Translated, among others, by Wilhelm Schlegel, written about by Mme de Staël, Camões appeared to the Romantics in all the dark glory of his turbulent and, as they depicted it, ultimately tragic life.

7. Although Osório was the son of a pioneer feminist, Ana de Castro Osório (1872–1935), his upbringing did not appear to influence his use of gendered personal pronouns in referring to generic or putative cultural agents: they are always male.

8. For an overview and a contemporary reassessment of Vieira's multifaceted literary and critical career, see Luís Forjaz Trigueiros, "Identidade humana e cultural de Afonso Lopes Vieira," in *Memórias da Academia das Ciências de Lisboa. Classe de Letras* 20 (1979): 333–50; and Fernando Cabral Martins's preface to the third edition of Vieira's "restitution" of the *Romance de Amadis* (Lisboa: Ulmeiro, 1984).

9. One curious aspect of Vieira's "resurrection" of the *Romance de Amadis* was his decision to eliminate all descriptions of battles and duels, whose presence in the text he attributed to the intervention of Castilian translators, and to maintain only the lyric parts, which according to him were assimilable to *saudade* and therefore truly "Portuguese" (Ramos 1994, 573). Regarding the question of the authorship of *Amadis* see the section on "O *Amadis de Gaula* e o problema da sua autoria" in the 1994 edition of Saraiva and Lopes's *História de Literatura Portuguesa* (97–98). The authors cite principal arguments in favor of Castilian or Portuguese provenance and conclude that the question has not so far been decisively settled.

Chapter 4. Canonizing Mariana

1. See Perkins 1992, 121–52 for a succinct discussion of historical contextualism as the dominant mode of explanation employed in modern literary history.

2. In his *Maneirismo e barroco na poesia lírica portuguesa*, Vítor Manuel de Aguiar e Silva offers a comprehensive historical overview of critical judgments and interpretations bestowed upon his object of study from the seventeenth century to the present (1971, 109–88). As his outline demonstrates, the nineteenth-century condemnation of *seiscentismo* had its sources in programmatic declarations of *Arcádia Lusitana*, with the seventh letter of Verney's *Verdadeiro método de estudar* (1746) as the most sustained and militant denunciation of Baroque aesthetics. Romantic literary historiography, without substantially modifying the thrust of earlier criticism, reformulated its terms by insisting on a causal relationship between literary phenomena and their contemporary social and political contexts.

3. The "Adamson" mentioned here refers to John Adamson, the author of *Memoirs of the Life and Writing of Luis de Camoens* (London: Longman, Hurst, Rees, Orme, and Brown, 1820). For an account of Higginson's involvement with Portugal and Portuguese literature, see George Monteiro, *The Presence of Camões*, 93–99.

4. As Teófilo wrote in his preface, "To our day Camões has been spared theoretical interpretation; smothered as he was by seventeenth-century commentators and embellished in nineteenth-century patriotic fantasies, a great deal of effort is necessary to recover him in his natural state" (quoted in Lourenço 1992, 139–40). Lourenço points out that Oliveira Martins had already offered, a year earlier, a properly "scientific" interpretation of Camões, which Teófilo resolutely chose to ignore in his own work.

5. See, for example, Alexandre Cioranescu, "La 'Religieuse portugaise' et 'tout le reste est littérature'," *Revue des Sciences humaines* 111 (juillet-septembre 1963): 317–27. More recently, the same line of argument was followed by Claude-Henri Frèches (1983, 220–21).

6. See also Vakil, "Representation of the 'Discoveries' and the Imaginary of the Nation in Portuguese Integralism," *Portuguese Studies* 11 (1995): 133–67.

7. See also Robert Johnstone, "The Impossible Genre: Reading Comprehensive Literary History," *PMLA* 107, 1 (1992): 26–37.

8. As Martha Hanna writes, "While Marianne served as the standard-bearer of Republicanism, Joan of Arc became, as a result of the conscious efforts of Action française, the icon of integral nationalism. . . . Unlike Marianne, whose unfortunate reputation as a

prostitute sullied her public image, the maid of Orléans was, according to popular legend, a girl of unimpeachable virtue" (1985, 216).

9. The "literate population" of the time was, of course, somewhat limited. According to data gathered in the 1920 census, it comprised some 80 percent of the population of Lisbon, but only about 50 percent in Porto and Santarém, and as little as 20 percent in the provincial districts of Leiria, Castelo Branco, and Beja (França 1992, 266–67).

10. Durão cites the following publications: Guy de Oliveira, *Sinopse actualizada da História da Literatura Portuguesa* (Lisboa, 1931); Albino Pereira Magno, *Sinopse da História da Literatura Portuguesa* (Lisboa, 1924); Berta V. de Almeida, *Breves noções de História da Literatura Portuguesa* (Lisboa, n.d.); Alfredo de Aguiar, *História de Literatura Portuguesa (resumo)* (Porto, 1932); José Agostinho, *História da Literatura Portuguesa* (Porto, 1927); and J. B. Bettencourt, *História Comparativa da Literatura Portuguesa* (Lisboa, 1923) as well as the more comprehensive and distinguished *Histórias* by Mendes dos Remédios (first published as *Literatura Portuguesa. Esboço histórico* in 1898, 6th edition in 1930) and Aubrey Bell (1922; Portuguese translation 1931).

11. On the artistic design of the exhibition, see França 1974, 216–22, and Portela 1982, 69–77.

12. "As cartas da Freira" in his *Estudos filosóficos e críticos* (Coimbra: Imprensa da Universidade, 1930), 359–64. In the same volume, see also the essay "A propósito de Amadis" (365–71), where Pimenta dissects the question of supposed Portuguese provenance of *Romance de Amadis*, criticizing zealous partisans of national authenticity for their lack of scholarly rigor ("The only position responsible critics can adopt is that of methodic doubt. Portuguese essence. . . . What Portuguese essence can there be in a thirteenth-century chivalrous romance, whose original version had never been printed and did not survive in a manuscript, and of which we know merely the Castilian version from 1508?" [369]). Pimenta returned to the question of Soror Mariana in his review of Albin Eduard Beau's article "Rainer Maria Rilke e as Cartas de Soror Mariana," where he resoundingly labeled the nun's letters as "one of the most appalling mystifications of world literature, one of its most shameless literary hoaxes" (*Diário de Notícias*, 13 August 1935).

13. See França 1974, 216–22, for an account of the battle waged between the "traditionalists" and the "modernists" over the design of the exhibition. In the end, among the twelve architects, nineteen sculptors, and forty-three painters who took part in its construction, some 20 percent were "academicians," 10 percent belonged to the "first Modernist generation" and 50 percent to the second (França, 221).

14. While this is certainly true with regard to Soror Mariana's contemporary presence in Portugal, voices insisting on the need to maintain open the issue of historic confirmation of her authorship may still occasionally be heard from such far-flung outposts of the Lusophone world as, for example, Southern California. See the Epilogue for a commentary on the recently published novel *Mariana* (1996) by the Portuguese-American writer, Katherine Vaz.

CHAPTER 5. GENDERING MARIANA

1. Writing (in 1870) well before Luciano Cordeiro's documentary discoveries, Teófilo mistakenly believed that the historical Mariana Alcoforado was a teenage girl at the

time when her love affair would have taken place ("the poor young nun would have been fifteen years old, eighteen at most. . . ." [189]).

2. Interestingly, at about the same time that assorted Portuguese Bergsonians-cum-*alcoforadistas* were busy painting a vitalist picture of Mariana Alcoforado, Rainer Maria Rilke conceived of a radically spiritual version of the Portuguese Nun who had "remade her pitifully uninteresting and inadequate fleshy lover into a pure internal possession" and achieved "an essence of love uncontaminated by warts and silly excuses" (Lipking, 162). See also Albin Eduard Beau, "Rainer Maria Rilke e as cartas da Sóror Mariana," *Boletim do Instituto Alemão* IV (1935): 1–18.

3. Aguiar's diagnosis is worth quoting in its entirety: "D. Fernando I was a moral invalid of the unstable type, with various associated deficiencies, among which the most conspicuous are characteristics of psychological masochism. D. Leonor Teles was a moral invalid of the inverted type, with hyperstesia of emotions and an exacerbated presence of characteristics proper to sadism" (1924, 192).

4. It is interesting to observe the manner in which Aguiar argued against the assertion, prevalent at the time, that physical masochism (distinct from his "masochismo moral") rarely occurred in women: for the Portuguese sexologist it was the woman's "proper and inborn tendency toward subjection" that constituted "a masochistic reflex"; as he rhetorically asked: "In how many cases does a woman victimized by her male companion find in his aggression a source of pleasure?" (47).

5. I have dealt with the invention of Violante de Cysneiros in "A mulher que nunca foi: para um retrato biográfico de Violante de Cysneiros." *Colóquio/Letras* 117/118 (1990): 103–14.

6. "Soror Mariana, a freira portuguesa por Luciano Cordeiro" in *Crónicas de Valentina* (Lisboa: Tavares Cardoso & Irmão, 1890) and "Cartas de amor. Soror Mariana—Mademoiselle de Léspinasse—George Sand" in *No meu cantinho* (Lisboa: A. M. Pereira, 1909).

7. It is difficult to resist the conjecture that the absent mother of Stegagno Picchio's genealogical metaphor might be the poet Florbela Espanca (1894–1930), often compared to Mariana Alcoforado, and until fairly recently neglected by most "serious" critics of modern Portuguese poetry (with the exception of some early, ambivalent appreciations by, notably, José Régio and Jorge de Sena). Formally unaffected by the Modernist turn and for the most part unabashedly "feminine" in their thematics, Florbela's sonnets provided a perhaps uncomfortable and ill-fitting antecedent to the works of the post–Second World War Portuguese women writers wishing to escape the stereotype and the stigma of "women's poetry."

8. I am grateful to Till Geiger and Hilary Owen for providing me with an English translation of the editors' preface to *Die Schwestern der Mariana Alcoforado*.

9. The issue of *Diário Popular* of 4 May 1972 (supplement "Quinta feira à tarde," n° 790, 5) published the response of the eminent literary critic Jacinto do Prado Coelho. The full roster of respondents included, among others, such major figures as Mário Dionísio, José Rodrigues Miguéis, Ruben A., Georg Rudolf Lind, and Jorge de Sena.

10. All quotes from *Novas Cartas Portuguesas* are based on the English translation by Helen R. Lane (1994). I have, however, modified it slightly in some cases for the sake of accuracy.

11. By contrast, *Novas Cartas Portuguesas* has not exercised an even remotely comparable influence in Portugal; even the book's importance to the present generation of

women writers "does not lie in its role as a direct influence or as an aesthetic model inspiring imitation" (Owen 1995, 186). However, as Hilary Owen contends, "in the light of the Three Marias' innovative practice, the subsequent development of women's fiction in Portugal enjoys an interesting, largely unexplored, paradigmatic relationship with polyphony in the feminine, the fragmentation of the female subject which we witness in *Novas Cartas*" (184).

EPILOGUE: THE MÉRTOLA WINDOW

1. For an exhaustive summary of the controversy surrounding "the Mértola window" and a conclusive restatement of the dominant *alcoforadista* position on the issue, see Fonseca, 70–81.

2. A screenplay entitled *Portuguese Love Letters* is however available for purchase to prospective producers from an online firm, Scripts-OnScreen (http://scripts-onscreen.com).

3. The poster may be viewed at http://www.blarg.net/~dr_z/Movie/Posters/nunamore.html.

Bibliography

Abreu, Graça. "'Le balcon d'où l'on voit Mertola': Le Mirage des points de repère dans les *Lettres portugaises.*" *Ariane* 6 (1988): 81–91.

Aguiar, Asdrúbal de. *Masoquismo psíquico de Soror Mariana Alcoforado.* Lisboa: Biblioteca Nacional, 1922.

———. *O "Rei Formoso" e a "Flor de Altura."* Separada do *Arquivo de Medicina Legal* (1922). Lisboa, 1924.

Ahmad, Aijaz. "Jameson's Rhetoric of Otherness and the 'National Allegory.'" *Social Text* 17 (fall 1987): 3–25.

Alcoforado, Mariana. *Cartas de Amor.* Rio de Janeiro: Imago, 1992.

Alcover, Madeleine. "Essai de Stemmatologie: la datation du manuscrit des *Lettres portugaises.*" *Papers on Seventeenth-Century French Literature* 12, 23 (1985): 621–50.

Almeida, Onésimo Teotónio. "A Questão da Identidade Nacional na Escrita Portuguesa Contemporânea." *Hispania* 74 (September 1991): 492–500.

———. "Portugal and the Concern with National Identity." *BHS* 71 (1994): 155–63.

Anderson, Benedict. *Imagined Communities.* Revised edition. London and New York: Verso, 1991.

Anderson, Perry. "Nation-States and National Identity." *London Review of Books* (9 May 1991): 3–8.

Arteaga, Alfred. Introduction: The Here, the Now. In *An Other Tongue. Nation and Ethnicity in the Linguistic Borderlands.* Edited by Alfred Arteaga. Durham: Duke University Press, 1994, 1–7.

Ashcroft, Bill, Gareth Griffiths, and Helen Tiffin, eds. *The Post-Colonial Studies Reader.* London and New York: Routledge, 1995.

Aveline, Claude. . . . *Et tout le reste n'est rien. La Religieuse portugaise avec le texte de ses lettres.* Paris: Mercure de France, 1986 [1951].

Barreno, Maria Isabel, Maria Teresa Horta, and Maria Velho da Costa. *Novas Cartas Portuguesas.* 3d ed. Lisboa: Moraes, 1982.

———. *New Portuguese Letters.* Translated by Helen R. Lane. New York and London: Readers International, 1994.

Barros, Thereza Leitão de. *Escritoras de Portugal.* 2 vols. Lisboa, 1924.

Barthes, Roland. *Mythologies*. Translated by Anette Lavers. New York: Hill and Wang, 1987.

Beauvoir, Simone de. *The Mandarins*. Translated by Leonard M. Friedman. Cleveland and New York: The World Publishing Company, 1956.

Beauvois, E. *La jeunesse du Maréchal de Chamilly*. Beaune: Arthur Batault, 1885.

Bell, Aubrey F. G. *Portuguese Literature*. Oxford: Clarendon Press, 1922.

Berman, Antoine. *The Experience of the Foreign. Culture and Translation in the Romantic Germany*. Translated by S. Heyvaert. Albany: SUNY Press, 1992.

Boerner, Peter, ed. *Concepts of National Identity. An Interdisciplinary Dialogue*. Baden-Baden: Nomos Verlagsgesellschaft, 1986.

Bordo, Susan. "Feminism, Postmodernism, and Gender-Scepticism." In *Feminism/Postmodernism*. Edited by Linda J. Nicholson. New York and London: Routledge, 1990, 133–56.

Botelho, José Maria de Sousa (Morgado de Mateus). "Notice bibliographique." In *Lettres portugaises. Nouvelle édition*. Paris: Firmin Didot, 1824.

Bouterwek, Frederick. [Friedrich] *History of Spanish and Portuguese Literature*. Vol. 2. Translated by Thomasina Ross. London: Boosey and Sons, 1823.

Braga, Teófilo. *Estudos da Edade Média*. Porto: Ernesto Chardron, 1870.

———. *História da Literatura Portuguesa*. Vol. 3, *Os Seiscentistas*. Lisboa: Imprensa Nacional–Casa da Moeda, 1984.

———. *Manual da história da literatura portuguesa*. Porto: Magalhães & Moniz, 1875.

Branco, Manuel Bernardes. *Portugal e os estrangeiros*. 2 vols. Lisboa: Livraria de A. M. Pereira, 1879.

———. *Portugal e os estrangeiros. Segunda parte*. 3 vols. Lisboa: Imprensa Nacional, 1893–95.

Brown, Marshall. "Contemplating the Theory of Literary History." *PMLA* 107, 1 (1992): 13–25.

Buell, Lawrence. "Literary History as a Hybrid Genre." In *New Historical Literary Study*. Edited by Jeffrey N. Cox and Larry J. Reynolds. Princeton: Princeton University Press, 1993, 216–29.

Buescu, Ana Isabel. "Um mito das origens da nacionalidade: o milagre de Ourique." In *A Memória da Nação*. Edited by Francisco Bethencourt and Diogo Ramada Curto. Lisboa: Sá da Costa, 1991, 49–69.

Buescu, Helena Carvalhão, coord. *Dicionário do Romantismo Literário Português*. Lisboa: Caminho, 1997.

Byron, Lord. *The Complete Poetical Works*. Edited by Jerome J. McGann. Vol. 2, *Childe Harold's Pilgrimage*. Oxford: Clarendon Press, 1980.

Cabral, Manuel Villaverde. "The Aesthetics of Nationalism: Modernism and Authoritarianism in Early Twentieth-Century Portugal." *Luso-Brazilian Review* 26, 1 (1989): 15–43.

Cardim, Luís. "Les *Lettres portugaises*. A propos de quelques documents récemment publiés." *Bulletin des Études Portugaises* 1 (1931): 161–73.

Carvalho, Francisco Freire de. *Primeiro Ensaio sobre História Literária de Portugal*. Lisboa, 1845.

Carvalho, Paulo Archer de. "Memória mítica da Nação—o caso do Integralismo Lusitano." *Vértice* 61 (Julho-Agosto 1994): 51–66.

Castelo Branco, Camilo. *Curso de Literatura Portuguesa.* Lisboa: Labirinto, 1986 [1876].

Castro, Augusto de. *A Exposição do Mundo Português e a sua finalidade nacional.* Lisboa: Empresa Nacional de Publicidade, 1940.

Chase-Dunn, Christopher. "Comparing World-Systems: Toward a Theory of Semiperipheral Development." *The Comparative Civilizations Review* 19 (1988): 29–66.

Coelho, Jacinto do Prado. *Originalidade da literatura portuguesa.* Lisboa: Instituto de Cultura e Língua Portuguesa, 1977.

Coelho, Maria Teresa Pinto. " 'Pérfida Albion' and 'Little Portugal': The Role of the Press in British and Portuguese National Perceptions of the 1890 Ultimatum." *Portuguese Studies* 6 (1990): 173–90.

Cordeiro, Luciano. *Sim Resposta aos que nos perguntam se queremos continuar a ser portugueses. Opúsculo anti-ibérico.* Lisboa, 1865.

———. *Soror Mariana, a freira portuguesa.* Lisboa: Livraria Ferin, 1888.

———. *Soror Mariana, a freira portuguesa.* 2d ed. Lisboa: Livraria Ferin, 1891.

———. *Questões coloniais.* Edited by A. Farinha de Carvalho. Lisboa: Vega, 1981.

Cortesão, Jaime. "Esboço crítico." In Soror Mariana, *Cartas de amor.* Lisboa, 1920.

Cuesta, Pilar Vázquez. *A língua a a cultura portuguesas no tempo dos Filipes.* Lisboa: Europa-América, 1988.

Dantas, Júlio. *Sóror Mariana (peça em 1 acto).* Lisboa: Portugal-Brasil, 1921 [1915].

DeJean, Joan. *Fictions of Sappho, 1546–1937.* Chicago: University of Chicago Press, 1989.

Deleuze, Gilles, and Félix Guattari. *Kafka: Toward a Minor Literature.* Translated by Dana Polan. Minneapolis: University of Minnesota Press, 1986.

Denis, Ferdinand. *Résumé de l'histoire littéraire du Portugal.* Paris: Leconte et Durey, 1826.

Durão, Paulo. "Compêndios de Literatura Portuguesa: As Cartas da Freira." *Brotéria* 16, 3 (Março 1933): 160–68.

Elísio, Filinto. *Obras.* Vol. 1. Lisboa, 1836–40.

Engelmeyer, Elfriede, and Renate Hess, eds. *Die Schwestern der Mariana Alcoforado. Portugiesische Schriftstellerinen der Gegenwart.* Berlin: edition tranvía, 1993.

Ezell, Margaret. "The Myth of Judith Shakespeare: Creating the Canon of Women's Literature." *New Literary History* 21, 3 (1990): 579–92.

Figueiredo, Fidelino de. *História da Literatura Clássica.* Revised 2d ed. Lisboa: Livraria Clássica, 1930.

Fishman, Joshua A. *Language and Nationalism.* Rowley, Mass.: Newbury House, 1973.

Fonseca, António Belard da. *Mariana Alcoforado. A Freira de Beja e as Lettres portugaises.* Lisboa, 1966.

Fox-Genovese, Elizabeth. "Literary Criticism and the Politics of New Historicism." In *The New Historicism.* Edited by Aram H. Veeser. New York and London: Routledge, 1989, 213–24.

França, José Augusto. *A Arte em Portugal no Século XX*. Lisboa: Bertrand, 1974.

———. *Os Anos 20 em Portugal*. Lisboa: Presença, 1992.

Frèches, Claude-Henri. "Une vision française de la féminité portugaise: les *Lettres portugaises* avec les *Responces* traduites en français." In *Les Rapports culturels et littéraires entre le Portugal et la France* (Actes du colloque Paris, 11–16 octobre 1982). Paris: Fondation Calouste Gulbenkian, 1983, 219–38.

Freyre, Gilberto. *Aventura e rotina*. Rio: José Olympio, 1953.

———. *The Portuguese and the Tropics*. Lisbon: Executive Committee for the Commemoration of the Fifth Centenary of the Death of Prince Henry the Navigator, 1961.

Garrett, João Baptista da Silva Leitão de Almeida. *Obras*. Porto: Lello & Irmão, 1966.

Geertz, Clifford. "Ideology as a Cultural System." In *The Interpretation of Cultures*. New York: Basic Books, 1973, 193–233.

Godard, Barbara. "Feminism and/as Myth: Feminist Literary Theory between Frye and Barthes." *Atlantis* 16, 2 (spring 1991): 3–21.

Gomes, Joaquim. Prefácio in *Cartas de Amor de Soror Mariana, seguidas das respostas*. Coimbra: França e Arménio Amado, 1914.

Green, F. C. "Who Was the Author of the *Lettres portugaises?*" *Modern Language Review* 21 (1926): 159–67.

Guillén, Claudio. *Literature as System. Essays Toward the Theory of Literary History*. Princeton: Princeton University Press, 1971.

Guilleragues, Gabriel-Joseph de Lavergne de. *Lettres portugaises, Valentins, et autres oeuvres*. Introduction, notes, glossaire et tables par F. Deloffre et J. Rougeot. Paris: Garnier, 1962

———. *Chansons et bons mots, Valentins, Lettres portugaises*. Edition nouvelle avec introduction, notes, glossaire par Frédéric Deloffre et Jacques Rougeot. Genève: Librairie Droz, 1972.

Guimarães, António. "Soror Mariana." *O Dia* 496, 498, 499 (2–5 June 1913).

Hanna, Martha. "Iconology and Ideology: Images of Joan of Arc in the Idiom of the Action française, 1908–1931." *French Historical Studies* 14, 2 (fall 1985): 215–39.

———. "Metaphors of Malaise and Misogyny in the Rhetoric of the Action Française." *Historical Reflections/Réflexions Historiques* 20, 1 (1994): 29–55.

Herzfeld, Michael. *Cultural Intimacy. Social Poetics in the Nation-State*. New York and London: Routledge, 1997.

Hesse, Carla. "Reading Signatures: Some Legal Contingencies of Female Authorship in France, 1750 to 1850." *Critical Matrix: Princeton Working Papers in Women's Studies* 2, 1–3 (spring 1986): 1–30.

Higginson, Thomas Wentworth. "Portugal's Glory and Decay." *North American Review* 173 (October 1856): 456–76.

Hobsbawm, Eric. *The Age of Empire, 1875–1914*. New York: Pantheon Books, 1987.

Hobsbawm, Eric, and Terence Ranger, eds. *The Invention of Tradition*. Cambridge: Cambridge University Press, 1983.

Hopkins, Terence K. "The Study of the Capitalist World-Economy. Some Introductory Considerations." In *World-Systems Analysis. Theory and Methodology*. Edited by Terence K. Hopkins, Immanuel Wallerstein, et al. Beverly Hills, London, and New Delhi: Sage Publications, 1982, 9–38.

Hopkins, Terence K., Immanuel Wallerstein, et al. *World-Systems Analysis. Theory and Methodology*. Beverly Hills, London, and New Delhi: Sage Publications, 1982.

Hyde, Douglas. "The Necessity for De-Anglicising Ireland." In *Language, Lore and Lyrics. Essays and Lectures*. Blackrock: Irish Academic Press, 1986, 153–70.

Jacquemond, Richard. "Translation and Cultural Hegemony: The Case of French-Arabic Translation." In *Rethinking Translation*. Edited by Lawrence Venuti. London and New York: Routledge, 1993, 139–58.

Jakobson, Roman. "On Linguistic Aspects of Translation." In *Language in Literature*. Cambridge, Mass., and London: The Belknap Press, 1987, 428–35.

Jameson, Fredrick. "Third-World Literature in the Era of Multinational Capitalism." *Social Text* 15 (fall 1986): 65–88.

JanMohamed, Abdul R., and David Lloyd, eds. *The Nature and Context of Minority Discourse*. Oxford: Oxford University Press, 1990.

Johnston, John. "Translation as Simulacrum." In *Rethinking Translation*. Edited by Lawrence Venuti. London and New York: Routledge, 1993, 42–56.

Jost, François. "L'Évolution d'un genre: le roman épistolaire dans les lettres occidentales." In *Essais de littérature comparée*. Vol. 2. Fribourg: Éditions Universitaires, 1968, 89–197.

Jusdanis, Gregory. "The Importance of Being Minor." *Journal of Modern Greek Studies* 8 (1990): 5–33.

Kamuf, Peggy. "Writing Like a Woman." In *Women and Language in Literature and Society*, edited by Sally McConnell-Ginet, Ruth Borker, and Nelly Furman. New York: Praeger, 1980, 284–99.

———. "Replacing Feminist Criticism." In *Conflicts in Feminism*, edited by Marianne Hirsch and Evelyn Fox Keller. New York and London: Routledge, 1990, 105–11.

Kamuf, Peggy, and Nancy K. Miller. "Parisian Letters: Between Feminism and Deconstruction." In *Conflicts in Feminism*. Edited by Marianne Hirsch and Evelyn Fox Keller. New York and London: Routledge, 1990, 121–33.

Kauffman, Linda S. *Discourses of Desire. Gender, Genre, and Epistolary Fictions*. Ithaca: Cornell University Press, 1986.

Larat, P. et J. "Les *Lettres d'une religieuse portugaise* et la sensibilité française." *Revue de la Littérature Comparée* 8 (1928): 617–39.

Leiner, Wolfgang. Review of *Lettres de la Religieuse portugaise*. Edited by Yves Florenne. *Papers on French Seventeenth-Century French Literature* 13, 1 (1980): 146–47.

Lipking, Lawrence. *Abandoned Women and Poetic Tradition*. Chicago: University of Chicago Press, 1988.

Lloyd, David. *Nationalism and Minor Literature*. Berkeley and Los Angeles: University of California Press, 1987.

———. *Anomalous States. Irish Writing and the Post-Colonial Moment*. Durham: Duke University Press, 1993.

Lopes, Adília. *O Marquês de Chamilly (Kabale und Liebe)*. Lisboa: Hiena, 1987.

Lourenço, Eduardo. "Prefácio." In Maria Velho da Costa, *Maina Mendes*. 2d ed. Lisboa: Moraes, 1977.

———. "Portugal-França ou a comunicação assimétrica." In *Les Rapports culturels et littéraires entre le Portugal et la France* (Actes du colloque Paris, 11–16 octobre 1982). Paris: Fondation Calouste Gulbenkian, 1983, 13–27.

———. *O Labirinto da Saudade*. Lisboa: Dom Quixote, 1992 [1978].

Macedo, Hélder. "Teresa and Fátima and Isabel". *Times Literary Supplement* (12 December 1975): 1484.

Machado, Álvaro Manuel. "La difficulté d'être portugais." *La Quinzaine littéraire* 73 (16–31 May 1969): 12–13.

Magalhães, Isabel Allegro de. *O Tempo das Mulheres*. Lisboa: Imprensa Nacional–Casa da Moeda, 1987.

Marques, A. H. Oliveira de. *História de Portugal*. 2 vols. Lisboa: Palas, 1972–74.

Matos, Sérgio Campos. *História, Mitologia, Imaginário Nacional. A História no Curso dos Liceus (1895–1939)*. Lisboa: Horizonte, 1990.

Matthews, Irene. Afterword in Marilene Felinto, *The Women of Tijucopapo*. Translated by Irene Matthews. Lincoln: University of Nebraska Press, 1994, 123–32.

Menand, Louis. "Eliot and the Jews." *The New York Review of Books* 43, 10 (6 June 1996): 34–41.

Michie, Helena. *Sororophobia. Differences Among Women in Literature and Culture*. Oxford: Oxford University Press, 1992.

Miller, Nancy K. "The Text's Heroine: A Feminist Critic and Her Fictions." In *Conflicts in Feminism*, edited by Marianne Hirsch and Evelyn Fox Keller. New York and London: Routledge, 1990, 112–20.

Monteiro, George. *The Presence of Camões. Influences on the Literature of England, America, and Southern Africa*. Lexington: University Press of Kentucky, 1996.

Monteiro, Gomes. "Vida e morte de Madre Mariana Alcoforado." *Arquivo Nacional* 472 (22 de Janeiro 1941): 56–57.

Montemor, Jorge de. *A Diana*. Em português de Afonso Lopes Vieira. Lisboa: Portugal-Brasil, 1924.

Montrose, Louis A. "Professing the Renaissance: The Poetics and Politics of Culture." In *The New Historicism*. Edited by Aram H. Veeser. New York and London: Routledge, 1989, 15–36.

Morgan, Robin. *Sisterhood Is Global*. New York: Anchor Press, 1984.

Múrias, Manuel. *O Seiscentismo em Portugal*. Lisboa, 1923.

Negreiros, José de Almada. *Obras Completas*. Vol. 6, *Textos de Intervenção*. Lisboa: Imprensa Nacional–Casa da Moeda, 1993.

Oliveira, Alice de. *Vida amorosa de Soror Mariana*. Lisboa: Parceria A. M. Pereira, 1944.

Oliveira, José Osório de. *Panorama da Literatura Portuguesa*. Lisboa: Ática, 1947.

Osório, João de Castro. *Florilégio das poesias portuguesas escritas em castelhano e restituídas à língua nacional*. Lisboa: Império, 1942.

Oulmont, Charles. Préface in *Cartas portuguesas/Lettres portugaises*. Lisboa: Bertrand, 1941.

Owen, Hilary. " 'Um quarto que seja seu': The Quest for Camões's Sister." *Portuguese Studies* 11 (1995): 179–91.

Pageaux, Daniel-Henri. *Imagens de Portugal na cultura francesa*. Lisboa: ICALP, 1983.

Parker, Andrew, et al., eds. *Nationalisms and Sexualities*. New York and London: Routledge, 1992.

Pereira, J. C. Seabra. *Do fim do século ao tempo de Orfeu*. Coimbra: Almedina, 1979.

Pereira, Leonardo. *As Cartas de Sóror Mariana*. Lisboa: Portugália, 1941.

Perkins, David. *Is Literary History Possible?* Baltimore: Johns Hopkins University Press, 1992.

Pimenta, Alfredo. "*Vida e morte de Madre Mariana Alcoforado*, de Manuel Ribeiro." *Diário de Notícias* (16 June 1941): 5.

Pintasilgo, Maria de Lurdes. Prefácio in Maria Isabel Barreno, Maria Teresa Horta, Maria Velho da Costa, *Novas Cartas Portuguesas*. Lisboa: Moraes, 1982, 11–28.

Portela, Artur. *Salazarismo e artes plásticas*. Lisboa: ICALP, 1982.

Pratt, Mary Louise. " 'Yo soy la Malinche': Chicana Writers and the Poetics of Ethnonationalism." In *Twentieth Century Poetry: From Text to Context*. Edited by Peter Verdonk. London: Routledge, 1993, 171–87.

Quadros, António. *A Ideia de Portugal na Literatura Portuguesa dos Últimos Cem Anos*. Lisboa: Fundação Lusíada, 1989.

Ramos, Rui. *A Segunda Fundação (1890–1926)*. Vol. 6 in *História de Portugal*. Directed by José Mattoso. Lisboa: Estampa, 1994.

Ribeiro, Cristina Almeida. "Cartas portuguesas." In *Biblos. Enciclopédia Verbo das Literaturas de Língua Portuguesa*. Lisboa & São Paulo: Verbo, 1995, 1004–07.

Ribeiro, José Silvestre. *Beja no anno de 1845*. Ed. facsimilada. Beja: Câmara Municipal, 1986 [1847].

Ribeiro, Manuel. "Soror Mariana Alcoforado." In Soror Mariana Alcoforado, *Cartas de amor*. Edição revista e prefaciada por Manuel Ribeiro. Lisboa: Guimarães, [1912].

———. *Vida e morte de Madre Mariana Alcoforado*. Lisboa: Sá da Costa, 1940.

Rocha, Andrée Crabbé. *A epistolografia em Portugal*. Coimbra: Livraria Almedina, 1965.

———. "Relações culturais luso-francesas. Do geral ao particular." In *Les Rapports culturels et littéraires entre le Portugal et la France* (Actes du colloque Paris, 11–16 octobre 1982). Paris: Fondation Calouste Gulbenkian, 1983, 373–82.

Rodrigues, A. Gonçalves. "Mariana Alcoforado. História e crítica de uma fraude literária." *Biblos* 11 (1935): 85–136.

Rosas, Fernando. *O Estado Novo (1926–1974)*. Vol. 7 in *História de Portugal*. Directed by José Mattoso. Lisboa: Estampa, 1994.

Sabugosa, Conde de. *Gente d'algo*. Lisboa: Portugal-Brasil, 1923 [1915].

Sadlier, Darlene J. *The Question of How. Women Writers and New Portuguese Literature*. Westport, Conn.: Greenwood Press, 1989.

Sampayo, Nuno de. "*Novas Cartas Portuguesas*." *A Capital*, suplemento "Literatura e Arte" (31 May 1972): 4.

Santos, F. Reis. "O movimento republicano e a consciência nacional." In *História do regimen republicano em Portugal*. Edited by Luís de Montalvor. Lisboa: Ática, 1930–32.

Saraiva, António José, e Óscar Lopes. *História da Literatura Portuguesa*. 14th edition. Porto: Porto Editora, 1987.

Saramago, Alfredo. *Convento de Soror Mariana Alcoforado*. Sintra: Colares, 1994.

Sardinha, António. "As 'Cartas' da freira." In *Da hera nas colunas*. Coimbra: Atlântida, 1929, 69–114.

Schleiermacher, Friedrich. "On the Different Methods of Translating." In *Translating Literature: The German Tradition*. Edited by André Lefevere. Assen & Amsterdam: Van Gorcum, 1977, 66–89.

Sequeira, Mattos. Prefácio in *Cartas de amor*. Lisboa: J. Rodrigues & Ca., 1925, 7–11.

Sérgio, António. "O Reino Cadaveroso, ou o problema da cultura em Portugal." In *Obras completas*. Vol. 2, *Ensaios*. Lisboa: Sá da Costa, 1972, 25–57.

Silva, Vítor Manuel de Aguiar e. *Maneirismo e barroco na poesia lírica portuguesa*. Coimbra: Centro de Estudos Românicos, 1971.

Sismondi, J. C. L. Simonde de. *Historical View of the Literature of the South of Europe*. Vol. 2. Translated by Thomas Roscoe. New York, 1827.

Sommer, Doris. "Irresistible Romance: The Foundational Fictions of Latin America." In *Nation and Narration*. Edited by Homi K. Bhabha. London and New York: Routledge, 1990, 71–98.

Sousa, Maria Leonor Machado de. Apresentação in . . . *como é diferente o amor em Portugal!* . . . Lisboa: Instituto da Biblioteca Nacional e do Livro, 1994.

Sousa Santos, Boaventura de. *Pela mão de Alice. O social e o político na pós-modernidade*. Porto: Afrontamento, 1994.

Spiering, M. *Englishness*. Amsterdam: Rodopi, 1992.

Spitzer, Leo. "The *Lettres Portugaises*." In *Essays on Seventeenth-Century French Literature*. Translated, edited, and introduced by David Bellos. Cambridge: Cambridge University Press, 1988, 355–83.

Spivak, Gayatri Chakravorty. "Can the Subaltern Speak?" In *Marxism and the Interpretation of Culture*. Edited by Cary Nelson and Lawrence Grossberg. Urbana: University of Illinois Press, 1988, 271–313.

Stegagno Picchio, Luciana. "Le nipoti di Marianna. Note sulla letteratura femminile in Portogallo." In *Gli abbracci feriti: poetesse portoghese di oggi*, a cura di Adelina Aletti. Milano: Feltrinelli, 1980, 5–11.

Stendhal. *De l'Amour*. Paris: Garnier, 1959.

Teixeira, Nuno Severiano. "Política externa e política interna no Portugal de 1890: o Ultimatum Inglês." *Análise Social* 23, 98 (1987): 687–719.

Tengarrinha, José. *História da imprensa periódica portuguesa*. Lisboa: Portugalia, 1988.

Vakil, AbdoolKarim A. "Nationalising Cultural Politics: Representations of the Portuguese 'Discoveries' and the Rhetoric of Identitarianism, 1880–1926." In *Nationalism and the Nation in the Iberian Peninsula*. Edited by Clare Mar-Molinero and Angel Smiths. Oxford and Washington, D.C.: Berg, 1996, 33–52.

Vaz, Katherine. *Mariana*. London: Flamingo, 1997.

Veeser, H. Aram, ed. *The New Historicism*. New York and London: Routledge, 1989.

Venuti, Lawrence. *The Translator's Invisibility. A History of Translation*. London and New York: Routledge, 1995.

Vidal, Duarte. *O processo das Três Marias*. Lisboa: Futura, 1974.

Vieira, Afonso Lopes. Prefácio in *Cartas portuguesas/Lettres portugaises*. Lisboa: Bertrand, 1941.

———. "Soror Mariana." In *Em demanda do Graal*. Lisboa: Portugal-Brasil, 1922, 253–59.

Wallerstein, Immanuel. *The Modern World-System*. Vol. 1. New York: Academic Press, 1974.

———. *The Capitalist World-Economy*. Cambridge: Cambridge University Press, 1979.

———. "World-Systems Analysis. Theoretical and Interpretative Issues." In Hopkins, Wallerstein, et al. *World-Systems Analysis. Theory and Methodology*. Beverly Hills, London & New Delhi: Sage Publications, 1982, 91–103.

———. "The Relevance of the Concept of Semiperiphery to Southern Europe." In *Semiperipheral Development. The Politics of Southern Europe in the Twentieth Century*. Edited by Giovanni Arrighi. Beverly Hills, London & New Delhi: Sage Publications, 1985, 31–39.

———. *Geopolitics and Geoculture*. Cambridge: Cambridge University Press, and Paris: La Maison des sciences de l'homme, 1991.

———. *After Liberalism*. New York: The New Press, 1995.

Wheeler, Douglas L. *Historical Dictionary of Portugal*. Metuchen, N.J.: The Scarecrow Press, 1993.

Wolff, Larry. *Inventing Eastern Europe. The Map of Civilization on the Mind of the Enlightment*. Stanford: Stanford University Press, 1994.

Woolf, Virginia. *A Room of One's Own*. New York: Harcourt Brace Jovanovich, 1981.

Index